PLAINS HISTORIES

John R. Wunder, *Series Editor*

American Outback

American Outback

The Oklahoma Panhandle in the Twentieth Century

Richard Lowitt

TEXAS TECH UNIVERSITY PRESS

T 123413

Book design by Mark McGarry

Library of Congress Cataloging-in-Publication Data
Lowitt, Richard, 1922–
American outback : the Oklahoma Panhandle in the twentieth century /
Richard Lowitt.
p. cm.—(Plains histories)
Summary: "Examines how inhabitants of the Oklahoma Panhandle throughout the
20th century used the semiarid lands that Kansas, Colorado, and New Mexico did not
want, and that Texas, after entering the Union as a slave state, could not have. Focuses
particularly on agriculture and production of natural gas"—Provided by publisher.
Includes index.
ISBN 0-89672-558-8 (hardcover : alk. paper)
1. Oklahoma Panhandle (Okla.)—History—20th century.
I. Title. II. Series.
F702.N6L69 2006   976.6'13053—dc22
2005020009
ISBN-13 978-89672-558-4

Printed in the United States of America
06   07   08   09   10   11   12   13 14 / 9   8   7   6   5   4   3   2   1

TS

Texas Tech University Press
Box 41037
Lubbock, Texas 79409–1037 USA
800.832.4042
ttup@ttu.edu
www.ttup.ttu.edu

For Paul Glad and Richard Nostrand
Fellow Tenants on the Back Forty

Contents

Illustrations

Acknowledgments

I STARTED RESEARCH on the Oklahoma Panhandle several years ago while awaiting readers' reports on a book-length manuscript. Once it was accepted and published, I devoted all my efforts to the four articles comprising this volume. Two appeared in the *Chronicles of Oklahoma* and two in *Agricultural History*. The article on Optima Dam appearing in the latter journal was originally delivered as a paper at an agricultural history conference at the University of Nevada in Reno. I am grateful to Mary Ann Blochowiak, editor of the *Chronicles of Oklahoma,* and the people handling permissions at the University of California Press, publisher of *Agricultural History,* for approving my request and allowing these four articles to appear in book form.

Numerous individuals, many in the course of casual conversations whose names remain unknown to me, aided, enhanced, and generally expanded my horizons by making the Oklahoma Panhandle one of the more exciting projects to command my attention. John Lovett, librarian in the Western History Collections at the University of Oklahoma played a major role in guiding me to collections, manuscript and photographic in particular.

The bulk of the pictures in this volume are located in the Western History Collections. In addition, the Oklahoma Geological Survey, also located at the University of Oklahoma, occasionally devoted issues to the Panhandle counties in its publication *Oklahoma Geology Notes*. The photograph of the helium plant in Cimarron County originally appeared on the cover of the May 1964 issue. It is reprinted with the approval of the Oklahoma Department of Commerce and Industry. And in the Government Documents division of the Bizzell Library, soil surveys of the Panhandle counties proved invaluable, as was the assistance of Mark Coe, a staff assistant, in locating these and other publications.

At the Historical Society in Oklahoma City, archivists in the Manuscripts Division directed me to its remarkable oral history collection, where I found numerous accounts of Dust Bowl days, while retired journalists who staffed the newspaper microfilm reading room suggested files that yielded stories unavailable in other collections. Nearby at the Oklahoma Department of Libraries Archives and Records Division, archivists introduced me to the files of various New Deal agencies that functioned in Oklahoma. Also in Oklahoma City, Robin Kicking Bird, an archivist at the *Oklahoman*, located the photographs of the pig farms. The photographs of the well heads were graciously provided by Gladys Renfro, curator of the Stevens County Gas and Historical Museum in Hugoton, Kansas. Stevens County, in southwestern Kansas, borders Texas County in the Panhandle. It overlays the enormous Hugoton natural gas field, which extends into both Texas and Beaver Counties.

As for individuals, I met three on the Norman campus whose interest in the Oklahoma Panhandle preceded mine and from whom I learned much through extended conversations. Neil Suneson, a geologist with the Geological Survey, provided me with a set of articles compiled for a class, among other things. These directed me to topics I needed to consider. Gary Gress, then a geography graduate student completing a dissertation on Oklahoma School Lands, many acres of which are in the Panhandle, alerted me to their significance. And then there is Jeff Alexander, with a newly minted PhD in geography, in whose battered pick-up truck I rode to spend several days touring the area (incidentally, it is Jeff who called the term "an American Outback" to my attention). In the public library at Texhoma, the Beaver County Historical Society in Beaver, the No Man's Land Historical Museum in Goodwell, and the Cimarron Heritage Center Museum in Boise City, librarians, curators, and others provided information and literature that greatly assisted my efforts. At the *Boise City News,* editor John Roseberry ferreted from the files a special edition devoted to the history of the area. People in the Housing Office at Panhandle State University in Goodwell put us up for a night in the dormitory. The next morning we had breakfast with the football team. Finally, I should mention the Black Mesa Bed and Breakfast near Kenton, where we received a splendid meal with most of the ingredients freshly picked from the nearby vegetable garden and where we discussed the Panhandle, past and present, on into the evening hours with our hosts, Monty Joe and Vicki Roberts.

*On the vast Great Plains, the tiny Oklahoma Panhandle
has been an American Outback.*

Plainsword

THE OKLAHOMA PANHANDLE is an odd creation. It's what happens when politics and geography collide. In fact, the entire state of Oklahoma does not look like a natural entity even though it does have the Red River to guide its southern boundary. If someone was trying to design a six-shooter of the kind featured in Walter Prescott Webb's classic, *The Great Plains,*[1] Oklahoma comes to mind with the Panhandle constituting the gun barrel.

What then of this Panhandle and its history? The Panhandle owes its geopolitical creation to the reduction of the Texas Republic to its current geographical borders upon statehood in 1845 and the creation of the Kansas Territory in 1854 by the Kansas-Nebraska Act. A sliver of land remained, nearly 6,000 square miles, to be attached to the state of Oklahoma in 1907.[2] Three counties were created: Cimarron, Texas, and Beaver. Cimarron refers to the river of the same name that meanders in and out of Kansas along the Panhandle's northern border. Beaver likewise borrows from Beaver Creek, a river of sorts that traverses the length of the Panhandle before flowing into the

northern branch of the Canadian River. Texas merely acknowl-
edges an affinity to an adjacent panhandle.

This term "panhandle" is a curious piece of Americana. There
are six recognized panhandles in the United States, three of them
on the Great Plains (Oklahoma, of course, and Texas and
Nebraska) and five of them in the West (add Idaho and Alaska),
with the sixth panhandle in Florida. Given that a panhandle is a
geographical attachment to a body of land, not surprisingly
defined as shaped like a pan's handle,[3] one might have expected
Massachusetts to have a panhandle or even Vermont or New
Hampshire to be panhandles of New England. Easterners must
not like the term. Of course, "panhandle" is not only a noun but
also a verb that means "to beg," and although begging is not generally seen as a positive attribute, particularly by panhandle natives
who tend to the conservative side of the social ledger, the Great
Plains panhandles have historically been places where the federal
government has generously provided vast resources in order to
help out resident farmers, ranchers, and oilmen in times of need.

The Oklahoma Panhandle is nearly a century old. It should
celebrate its centennial in 2007. It has always been sparsely populated, and that trend continues. Less than 30,000 people live in
its three counties, making the population approximately 5 per-
sons per square mile. Cimarron County has the smallest population of any county in the state of Oklahoma. Thirteen towns are
incorporated in the Panhandle, and only six have a population of
more than 1,000. The largest town is Guymon, county seat of
Texas County. Nearby Goodwell serves as the location of Panhandle State University and the No Man's Land Museum. That

the Panhandle might have been perceived as an afterthought to the map makers, people in the region prior to Oklahoma becoming a state asked for admission as a state of their own. They attempted to form "Cimarron Territory," with Beaver City, the current county seat of Beaver County, as the proposed capital and even elected senators and a representative. While it showed a certain spunk and verve, the independent entity of Cimarron and her prospective citizens had to be content with being attached to Oklahoma Territory.[4] Isolated, infrequently settled, a driven-through place, and basically unknown to a vast number of Americans and even to eastern Oklahomans, it is understandable why it is dubbed an American Outback.

The High Plains are very flat in the Oklahoma Panhandle. Its grasslands represent some of the better prairies of the heartland, so it is not surprising that bison once thrived in the region and cattle still do today. The land itself is fertile although it requires dryland farming techniques or irrigation to be profitable for farming. And the Hugoton Gas Field, largest in the United States, crosses through both Texas and Cimarron counties. The small town of Keyes was the site of one of the largest helium processing plants in North America.[5] Nature has not been neglectful in providing for the region.

The twentieth century, basically the only era of the Panhandle's existence, brought both opportunity and catastrophe. Opportunity came first in the form of high cattle prices and later in high wheat prices; then catastrophe struck in the form of drought and continued for seven straight years during the 1930s. Such extremes are certainly attached to Plains history, and the folks of the Panhandle have had their fair share of ups and downs.[6]

Mid-America University, a 1970s creation of Nebraska Educational Television and the Nebraska Humanities Council, produced a six-part video series on the history of the Great Plains, and the fifth film featured a visit to Guymon and the Oklahoma Panhandle. *The Heirs to No Man's Land* begins by following a cattle truck into Guymon as a Willie Nelson song blares on the local radio station. The viewer is taken through reflections by Panhandle residents who ponder the meanings of the past. A. P. "Red" Atkins recalls that after World War I, ranch land was easily available, so he, even as a new college graduate, was able to start up. His son and grandson assert that no other time, including the present, has existed in Panhandle history when such opportunities were available. While the cattle market fell shortly thereafter, Red remembers the introduction of the first combines, pulled by sixteen to twenty horses, and the corresponding good wheat prices. Willie B. Rolls, a single octogenarian, opines on how electricity brought a revolution; two theaters came to grace Guymon's business district, and farmers sought to obtain single engine planes. But then came the Depression and, even worse, the drought, which resulted in no wheat crops from 1931 to 1938. The dust bowl conditions, residents agreed, were even worse than the economic depression. Without grass, no cattle herds could be maintained. Without moisture, no crops could be cultivated. Still Panhandle residents proved plucky. They helped each other out, kept businesses afloat with extensive credit, and lamented when some residents decided they had to move. When Franklin Delano Roosevelt declared a bank holiday on March 3,

1933, Guymon banker G. R. Gear didn't think they needed to close until the Oklahoma attorney-general threatened to send the state militia to the Panhandle. Gear complied and closed the bank for two weeks, but he gave his depositors notice so they could withdraw what they needed. Yes, these western Oklahomans had a creative streak.[7]

The twentieth century has not been a favorite time for historians of the American West, and the number of talented historians of the Great Plains who have taken on the task of chronicling this modern era can be counted on two hands. One of the very best is Richard Lowitt, author of this history of the Oklahoma Panhandle. Lowitt is known for a number of excellent biographical volumes of prominent twentieth-century Plains leaders. Perhaps his most lauded effort is a three-volume biography of George Norris, Nebraska senator, Progressive leader, and New Dealer.[8] Also benefiting from Lowitt's pen have been New Mexican politician Bronson Cutting[9] and Oklahoma's own populist Fred Harris.[10] Particular note should also be called to Lowitt's groundbreaking survey, *The New Deal and the West*,[11] and his most recent book on the Standing Bear trial, co-authored with Valerie Sherer Mathes.[12]

Thus, to have a historian of this stature turn his attention to writing a modern history of the Oklahoma Panhandle is of significant importance, and we are honored to have this book as part of the new series, Plains Histories, published by Texas Tech University Press.

JOHN R. WUNDER
Lincoln, Nebraska, 2006

American Outback

The Oklahoma Panhandle—A Cross Section of the Southern High Plain

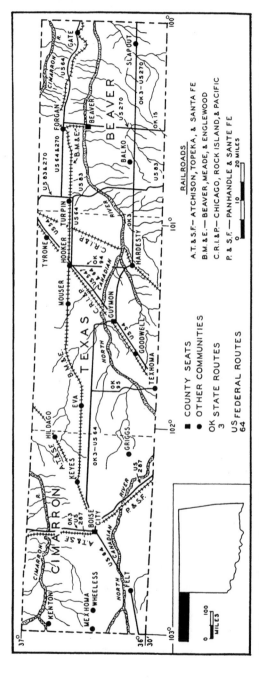

The Oklahoma Panhandle at mid-century. From "The Oklahoma Panhandle:A Cross Section of the Southern High Plains,"
Economic Geography 36 (1).With permission from Clark University.

Introduction

AMERICA'S OUTBACK, the unforgiving land of the Oklahoma Panhandle, emerged during the twentieth century as a prosperous yet risky place. To settle and to stick there was an achievement. One such settler who proved up a homestead with her husband was Caroline Henderson, a remarkable literary talent whose collected writings provide an intimate view of modern Plains life. A graduate of Mt. Holyoke College, Henderson and her husband, Will, sustained themselves on their family farm from 1907 until shortly before her death in 1966.

Although Caroline Henderson never published a major book, she depicted rural life from her family's vantage point near Eva in Texas County, the epicenter of the Oklahoma Panhandle, with insight and care for over half a century in a handful of published articles and a multitude of letters. Caroline, Will, and their child witnessed the tumultuous events that made farming a hazardous venture on the southern Plains during the last century. She portrayed the change of seasons, relished the arrival of birds in the spring, and expressed her love for this harsh land in prose that attracted a national audience. Her commentary, as Alvin Turner observed, "offers unique insights into the history of the Great Plains, where pioneering conditions, environmental threats, and relative isolation persisted through much of the twentieth century."[1]

The Henderson family arrived in the Panhandle in 1907, the year of Oklahoma's statehood. Comprising land that Kansas, Colorado, and New Mexico did not want, and that Texas, after entering the Union as a slave state, could not have. This geographic anomaly, 165 miles long and only 35 miles wide, extended above the 36°30' line of demarcation that separated slave from free territory, as set forth by the Missouri Compromise in 1820. This area, which belonged to no individual or group of individuals, was dubbed "No Man's Land" and served as a haven for desperadoes and villains in the time before Oklahoma's statehood. It was not subject to laws, rules, or regulations, nor was it affiliated with any organized governmental entity until 1890, when the Panhandle was included in the newly created Oklahoma Territory. An effort to create a separate "Territory of Cimarron" in 1887 came to naught.

After Oklahoma achieved statehood, "No Man's Land" next attracted national attention in the 1930s, when drought on the southern Plains placed it at the heart of the Dust Bowl. Limelight then caught the Panhandle in the 1950s, when it led the world in production of natural gas, and again in the 1990s, when it became home to massive corporate pig farms. This history of the Oklahoma Panhandle, examined in the chapters that follow, is an integral part of the history of the Great Plains.

Covering one-fifth of the land area of the United States, the Great Plains extends from the eastern slope of the Rocky Mountains to roughly the 98th meridian, an arbitrary demarcation line supposedly separating tall-grass from short-grass country, where normal rainfall is twenty inches or less. The Great Plains cover a distance of about 750 miles from east to west. The Plains stretch north to include portions of the Canadian Prairie Provinces and south into northern Mexico, a distance of more than 1,600 miles. Devoid of trees in most places, except in river bottoms, the Great Plains accounts for about two-fifths of the cropland and one-half of the grassland pasture in the United States. It is the peculiar domain of the windmill, partly because of climatic conditions, partly because of the need of water for irrigation, and in large part because of the lack of constant streams to supply water for stock. Its largely rural and agricultural population owns few taxable resources other than agricultural real estate.

The Great Plains differ from the humid East and the far West in terms of climate, soil, vegetation, and native animal life. Its flatness, treelessness, semi-aridity, and preeminence as an agricultural producer help give the region a sense of unity. For a portion of the twentieth century, when the Great Plains experienced drought, dust, and depopulation, it endured a hinterland status. Yet for a good portion of its history, Americans viewed the Great Plains as a transit area going "from nowhere to somewhere." The Platte River Road continues as the major, but not the only, route across the Great Plains since the days of the Mormon and Oregon Trails, the overland stagecoach lines, the Pony

Express, the Union Pacific Railroad, the Lincoln Highway, and Interstate 80. Other more limited thoroughfares, such as the Santa Fe Trail, with its Cimarron cutoff through the Oklahoma Panhandle, served a similar role in bringing people and goods to the destinations beyond the Great Plains. In the Panhandle itself, a direct, paved highway connecting it to Oklahoma City was not constructed until the late 1920s.

To people in transit, the Great Plains was a foreboding place, and it remains so to this day. It is relatively flat and treeless. The scarcity of rainfall produces plants able to withstand long dry spells and grasses able to retain moisture. Although it is a country of violent weather prone to thunderstorms, tornadoes, blizzards, and droughts over the course of a year, the Great Plains also contains fertile lowlands and thriving communities. Its history records pre-contact indigenous cultures and competition between European powers and American interests for its resources, as well as sporadic violence and warfare. Yet for all its human history and cultural diversity, the Great Plains remains relatively uniform and unchanged in physical environment. Human beings had to adapt their ways to suit this region that has, at different times with some validity, been called "a treeless destitute grasshopper country," "the Great American Desert," "the pastoral garden of the world," "the floor of the sky," and "the bread basket of the world," among others.

One can understand the conflicting imagery by briefly noting aspects of its history. Between 1914 and 1919, millions of acres of native grasses were turned under. Unusually wet years in the

1920s yielded bumper crops and further conversion of grassland to wheat. Drought in the 1930s exposed millions of those acres to wind. Also during those years, increasing tenancy led to population instability, neglect of improvements, low living standards, soil depletion, overgrazing, and a decline in community life. As the credit of taxing units declined, debts increased, and schools and public services suffered severely. At the same time, the specter of the Dust Bowl played a prominent role as New Deal agencies encouraged the development of contoured and terraced fields to limit water erosion and the planting of shelterbelts to retard wind velocity. And above all, people on the Great Plains learned that maintaining a grass cover on their land was a necessary first step in curbing erosion. In part due to these programs, the region became dependent on the national government for the maintenance of economic stability.

When severe drought reappeared in the 1950s, dust storms were few and far between, thanks in part to tillage practices implemented in the 1930s. The postwar years witnessed tremendous changes in the economy of large portions of the Great Plains. Advanced technology permitted widespread tapping of the Ogallala Aquifer, thereby providing water for a dry land. Natural gas and oil discovered and brought on line in the 1950s powered the irrigation systems that allowed for the cultivation of dry lands and sustained huge farms. Non-irrigated lands continue to function as range for almost half the livestock in the nation, with feedlots and packing plants producing beef and, more recently, pork for distant markets.

The availability of water allowed for the expanded production of cantaloupes and sugar beets in Colorado and the introduction of cotton in West Texas. Corn and grain sorghums supported cattle and pig operations, while wheat allowed the region to maintain its status as the world's leading bread basket.

The Ogallala Aquifer, a huge water reservoir underlying about 174,000 square miles in eight states but mostly in Nebraska, Kansas, Oklahoma, and Texas, is composed primarily of unconsolidated, poorly sorted silt, sand, gravel, and clay. It is a finite resource that recharges very slowly. In addition, the volume of drainable water varies from state to state. Nebraska has almost two-thirds of the groundwater, followed by Texas with 12 percent and Oklahoma with 3.5 percent. Since the issue of groundwater depletion is central to the economic productivity of the Great Plains, every effort is made to use water efficiently. By the 1970s farmers used center pivot irrigation; they also practiced drip irrigation and furrow irrigation using rubber, plastic, or aluminum tubes. In some instances, underground concrete pipes replaced the ditches. New pumping techniques created a golden age of irrigation and an integrated agribusiness economy. How long it will be sustained is an open question, and prognostications are being continually revised. But for the present, mechanized irrigation from Ogallala water has turned the old Dust Bowl into a prosperous, productive agricultural empire.

Except for use of Ogallala water for oil recovery, the Great Plains are generally free of cumbersome water pollution. The absence of major cities and little heavy industry mean that most

available water is devoted to agriculture. But weather still plays a
role and its extremes frequently occur at times critical to crop
production. The region is exposed to the strongest, steadiest
winds in America, with the average velocity in the Texas and
Oklahoma panhandles at twelve to fourteen miles per hour. A
good rainfall ensures bumper crops, and a severe drought means
unprofitable ones, especially in areas unable to tap underground
water. Overall, the end of the twentieth century reflects this history, as do the letters of Caroline Henderson discussed at the
outset of this introduction. Here, too, human enterprise clashed
with elemental forces of nature while adapting the use of the
land.

An American Outback

The Oklahoma Panhandle, 1907 to 1930

ONLY 168 miles long and 34 ½ miles wide with more than 3.6 million acres, the Oklahoma Panhandle enjoyed a long and colorful history before it became part of Oklahoma's territory in 1890 and entered the Union as three counties in 1907. Like the Australian Outback, it was, and still is, a sparsely populated area with few roads, sporadically settled areas, and long hauling distances. Drought plagued both Australia and the Panhandle and seriously affected the pastoral industry, primarily range cattle. Australia has cattle stations; the Panhandle has large ranches, although by the 1920s the area balanced grazing with large acreages devoted to wheat and grain sorghums. Both areas have noticeable sand dunes and sandy streams that are reduced to trickles during the dry season. In both outbacks, cattle can graze up to ten miles from water but are much more likely to stay within a radius of three to five miles. Rainfall provides surface water that may last for several months in water holes (Australian) or playas (Panhandle). Much of the territory in both outbacks is level except for broken country along the streams. Australia has some surrounding mountains ranges. In the western end of the Panhandle, the Cimarron River flows through a broad canyon, tapering off from the Black Mesa, the highest point in Oklahoma, at just 4,973 feet above sea level. In addition, both areas have to ship to distant markets and face the risk of severe weather.[1]

Spain, Mexico, and Texas successively claimed the Oklahoma Panhandle before it became part of the United States. Falling north of 36°30' north latitude, the Panhandle did not become part of Texas when it agreed to relinquish all claims to lands above the 1820 Missouri Compromise line once the Compromise of 1850 was adopted. This same measure established the New Mexico Territory with its eastern boundary at 103° west longitude, starting at the 32nd parallel and running north to the 37th parallel, just south of the Arkansas River in present-day Colorado. The Kansas-Nebraska Act defined the northern boundary of the Panhandle in 1854. This measure initially set the southern boundary of the Kansas Territory at 36°30' north latitude. In its final form, however, the Kansas-Nebraska Act effectively repealed the Missouri Compromise and defined 37° north latitude as the Kansas Territory's southern boundary. Thus, the southern boundary of the Panhandle had been created in 1850 by extending the Missouri Compromise line into Texas, while its northern boundary was created by a repeal of the line in 1854. When Kansas attained statehood in 1861, it designated the 102nd rather than the 103rd meridian as its western boundary and ceded back to the federal government its territorial lands west of that meridian, which promptly became part of the newly defined Colorado Territory. Consequently the Oklahoma Panhandle and later, in 1907, Cimarron County were bordered by four states: Colorado, Kansas, New Mexico, and Texas, a unique position applicable to no other county in the nation.[2]

This land remained outside the jurisdiction of any state until

1890, thereby earning it the name of "No Man's Land": it had no law officers, no land agency for filing claims or registering property deeds, no post office, no courthouse, and no institutional apparatus. Cattle drivers, sheepherders, outlaws, and settlers, who carved out farms, ranches, and towns to which they could not claim title, inhabited the area. Pioneers banded together to meet the challenges imposed by a brutal environment and outlaws in a region beyond the pale. Population in the Panhandle began to increase after 1880 because many settlers believed the area to be within the Cherokee Outlet, which was part of the public domain and open to homesteading. However, by the end of the 1880s, Interior Department rulings made it abundantly evident that the Cherokee Outlet did not extend beyond the 100th meridian. These rulings, combined with severe weather, curbed the invasion of settlers, and the population dwindled from as many as 14,000 people in the mid-1880s to less than 3,000 by 1890, roughly the same population as in 1880. During the 1880s the area was called the Cimarron Territory, and a provisional government with no legal sanctions was created. The Organic Act of 1890 placed the Panhandle under the new Oklahoma Territorial Administration, ending decades of legal uncertainty. With the establishment of Oklahoma Territory, the provisional government was lost, and the Panhandle was called Beaver County. With statehood in 1907 the Panhandle was divided into three counties that were among the largest in Oklahoma: Cimarron, Texas, and Beaver.[3]

Thus the development of the Oklahoma Panhandle was not

formally launched until the early twentieth century. Although
land use and climatic conditions were similar to those in bordering Texas and Kansas as well as in the more limited High Plains
areas of Colorado and New Mexico, development of the Panhandle occurred decades later than in those surrounding areas.
In addition, the Panhandle was largely cut off geographically and
historically from the rest of Oklahoma, awarding it a degree of
exceptionalism, an outback status, that merits examination as a
separate entity.

In Oklahoma the High Plains slope gently from a height of
nearly 5,000 feet in the extreme western part of the Panhandle to
about 2,000 feet at its eastern end in Beaver County. Near Black
Mesa in the far northwestern corner of the state, the Cimarron
River has cut a deep valley, forming ledges of brown sandstone.
With this exception, very little rock is evident on the surface of
the High Plains. In most places, the surface is so level that one
can see for ten to twenty miles in every direction. In 1907, when
the territory was officially organized as a state, only the occasional farm, ranch house, or solitary windmill broke the dull
monotony of the level plain.

Into this flat plain several streams have cut their broad and
shallow valleys. However, only the North Canadian, known in
the region as the Beaver River, travels the entire length of the
Panhandle. The river is formed in southwestern Cimarron
County by the junction of two creeks, then flows eastward, dipping into Texas for a short distance before returning to the
southwest corner of Texas County, flowing past Guymon and

Beaver, and leaving the Panhandle just south of Gage in northeast Beaver County.

The Cimarron River, rising in northeastern New Mexico, flows east through a broad canyon and enters Oklahoma in the northwest corner of Cimarron County. It quickly winds its way out of the area into Colorado, then Kansas, and cuts across the northeast corner of Beaver County, flowing further into Oklahoma. The valleys along the main streams are from one to three miles wide. However, the streams are sand choked and subject to sudden rises of floodwaters caused by cloudbursts; most of the water falling on the surface never reaches any drainage system. Water that the ground does not absorb or the wind or sun does not evaporate usually runs into shallow depressions known as playas, buffalo wallows, or, if large enough, lakes.

Stunted cottonwood, willow, or elm trees along with a few dwarfed pines and cedars are occasionally found along the shallow streams in the sandstone hills and on the slopes of Black Mesa. Otherwise, no native timber or tall grasses are evident in the Panhandle or on the High Plains in general. Instead, the ground everywhere was initially covered with a carpet of buffalo and mesquite grasses.

Much of the Panhandle began as cattle country with many herds grazing and an occasional cowboy riding the range. Early settlers usually constructed sod houses or dugouts as their residences. By the time of America's entrance into the First World War, cattle were yielding rangeland to wheat. In short, despite the four-line statement in the 1890 Bureau of the Census report that "there can hardly be said to be a frontier line," frontier living and pioneering was the rule and not the exception in the Oklahoma Panhandle in 1907.[4]

Climate is another factor that determines life on the High Plains. The weather is subject to sudden changes in temperature and severe wind gusts. During the summer the temperature climbs to more than one hundred degrees Fahrenheit, but because of low humidity it is not excessively oppressive, and the nights are usually cool. Occasionally winter temperatures drop as low as twenty degrees below zero Fahrenheit during blizzards. The last killing frost usually occurs in late April and the first around the twentieth of October, leaving a frost-free season of about 180 days. However, because of a slightly higher elevation and other factors, conditions in Cimarron County are always a bit more severe than in the other two counties.

Approximately two-thirds of the annual rainfall occurs from May to September; about one-third occurs as light rains that add little if any moisture to the subsoil. Heavy downpours are, however, not unknown, and severe flooding has wrought devastation at times. And, of course, the amount and distribution of precipitation has a direct bearing on agriculture; low annual rainfall makes the conservation and utilization of moisture an important factor in crop production.

Within a decade of the Panhandle becoming part of Oklahoma, wheat, sown in the fall near the end of the rainy season, became the principal crop. Wheat passes through the comparatively dry winter in a semi-dormant stage and matures early in the summer aided by late spring rains. Grain sorghums and broomcorn, the other significant crops, are drought resistant, utilize the summer moisture, and mature despite periods of drought and hot, dry winds. In the Panhandle through the first decades of the twentieth century, as elsewhere on the High Plains, dry farming was the rule, and wheat, requiring little effort by the farmer prior to harvesting, was an ideal crop. On farms where livestock grazed and crops were diverse, more winter work was necessary. Although destructive hailstorms occurred practically every summer, they were generally localized. Hot, dry winds did more damage. Moisture evaporated from leaves faster than the roots could supply them, and the porous, sandy soil retained little moisture. Hot winds curtailed crop yields more often than lack of rainfall.

As would be expected, early settlers usually sought lands along the Beaver River and the several streams. And, as already noted, raising cattle was the main endeavor. The breaks along the streams provided pasture and were divided into several large ranches. The plains were used for grazing cattle when the intermittent playas contained water. It was not until the 1950s that farmers discovered that an abundant supply of good water could be secured from the plains by drilling to a depth ranging from 150 to 200 feet. Once wells were drilled and windmills installed, more land could be used for grazing. Grass in the breaks was then saved for winter pasture because the broken land provided shelter and taller grasses. Although these grasses were rarely covered completely with snow, a few severe winters taught ranchers the benefit of having feed to supplement the native pastures. Initially, native hay that grew along the stream bottoms was cut and stacked; alfalfa later provided a feed crop.

As settlement in the Panhandle progressed, homesteaders began to break the native sod and grow crops. Breaking sod was the only work necessary to cultivate the land; practically no brush or shrubs grew to interfere with farming. As a result, the amount of cultivated land exploded until it came to include a very large portion of the three counties. The new settlers had to learn through experience which crops could adapt to these semi-arid conditions. Most of them kept a few cattle and left part of their holdings in pasture. With expanding agricultural production and the introduction of power machinery, farmers adopted large-scale operations. Farms were originally plotted in units of 160 acres, but by 1930 many ranged from 480 to 640 acres and some wheat farms reached a maximum size of four to five sections.[5]

The primary engine for change in the Panhandle was the railroad, which opened the region to settlement, accelerated the creation of communities, and prompted enhanced agricultural development so much so that the sod buster soon superseded the rancher in land use. The first railroad, the Rock Island, entered the region before statehood in 1901, when it resumed construction on a route from Liberal, Kansas, southwestward through Texas County into Texas and New Mexico, en route to California. By tracking this route, Texas County gained a lead over Beaver and Cimarron counties that it never relinquished. Beaver County did not have a railroad until almost a decade later, and Cimarron County had to wait until 1925. Before the railroad, farmers had to load their produce into wagons headed for elevators and terminals in neighboring Kansas and Texas. Texhoma, Hooker, Tyrone, Goodwell, and Guymon—the county seat and soon the largest community in the Panhandle—experienced growth beyond that of other settled areas. The stretch of Rock Island between Guymon and Dalhart, Texas, was one of the longest stretches of perfectly straight railroad tracks in the nation. Aspiring villages not included on the railroad route were usually headed for oblivion.

Legal problems thwarted the arrival of further railroads. Section 9 of Article IX of the Oklahoma constitution contained a provision prohibiting any transportation company organized under its laws from consolidating with any similar company organized under the laws of any other state. Six years passed before this provision was repealed. After a proposed amendment passed the state legislature, a referendum defeated it in April 1911. After further failures, the proposed amendment won in the referendum of August 5, 1913. Beaver and Cimarron counties could then encourage railroads to construct lines within their borders so that produce and freight would no longer have to be moved in wagons to stations on the Rock Island line, to Englewood, Kansas, on the Santa Fe line, or to the town of Shattuck in western Oklahoma.

In 1912, before the approval of the referendum, the Wichita Falls and Northwestern Railroad entered the new town of Forgan and provided service to Beaver County. As railroad towns close to the Kansas line, Knowles and Gate were assured a future. To avoid isolation and economic deprivation, Beaver City residents raised funds for the construction of a seven-mile spur to Forgan, which was known as the Beaver, Meade, and Englewood Railroad. Almost thirteen years later the Santa Fe Railroad entered Cimarron County, and Boise City celebrated its arrival on October 2, 1925. By mid-November, the line was completed to Felt, southwest of Boise City, en route to New Mexico. By the end of the 1920s, every county seat in the Panhandle was shipping carloads of cattle and grains to out-of-state markets while receiving carloads of supplies and equipment. In addition, the Beaver, Meade, and Englewood line was pushing westward from Forgan through Hooker and into Keyes in the eastern part of Cimarron County, where it joined with the east-west line of the Santa Fe route. Indications suggested that the Beaver, Meade, and Englewood line would also become part of the Rock Island or the Missouri, Kansas, and Texas Railroad. In 1937, a Santa Fe line from Amarillo, Texas, to Las Animas, Colorado, was completed, providing Cimarron County with yet another market outlet.

By the mid-1930s, the Panhandle had two lines of the Rock Island through Texas County serving all three counties: the Missouri, Kansas, and Texas Railroad, which had absorbed both the Wichita Falls and Northwestern Railway, and the Beaver, Meade, and Englewood Railroad. In addition, the Santa Fe had crossing lines in Cimarron County. While the railroads contributed immeasurably to the growth and prosperity of the Panhandle through the 1920s, construction was decades behind lines in neighboring Kansas, Texas, and Colorado, further contributing to the exceptionalism of the Oklahoma Panhandle.[6]

Texas County, having the early transportation advantage, quickly capitalized on its opportunities. Established in 1901, Guymon was the leading shipping and commercial center of the Panhandle by 1905. The railroad also led to a population increase in the three counties from less than 5,000 to more than 35,000 people within a five-year period (1902–1907). Within this same period, Guymon had grown from about 1,300 to about 1,500 people. By the time Oklahoma obtained statehood, Texas County had forged to the forefront as a great agricultural section, although many cattle were still shipped from Guymon. Moreover, as ranches gave way to farming operations, graded shorthorn cattle replaced longhorns. Farmers who kept small herds of beef breeds along with increasing numbers of dairy cows replaced ranchers. This pattern soon spread to other counties, and the combination of farming with raising stock, dairy cows, and poultry became the basis of the rural economy.[7]

The Rock Island Railroad also brought with it a new wave of settlers, many from the South, who quickly secured every acre of available land in the county. Called "pumpkin rollers" by the older settlers, many planted cotton. Their fields soon produced from one-half to three-fourths of a bale per acre. Cotton, however, never caught on as a leading crop. Prior to the construction of a gin in the county, the crop had to be hauled out of state. And once a gin was constructed, the cost of shipping cotton to market was almost prohibitive. The pumpkin rollers shifted gradually from cotton to wheat, a more profitable venture. The specialists at the Panhandle Agricultural Institute established in 1909 at Goodwell (a station on the Rock Island line in Texas County) assisted the pumpkin rollers and all Panhandle settlers in finding new crops and farming methods suited to the region.

At the outset, the county yielded surprisingly diverse crops, attributable in good part to the recent rush of settlers. Panhandle cantaloupes were said to rival those produced in Rocky Ford, Colorado, in both flavor and sweetness, and they were ready for market at least two to three weeks before the Colorado product. In 1907, nearly one hundred cars of cantaloupes were shipped to market. In 1908, boosters were envisioning Texas County as a great producer of sugar beets. With cotton gins operating in Hooker and Tyrone by 1908, it was not unusual to see cotton and corn growing side by side. In addition, vegetables of all kinds were produced in great abundance on small acreages. Though much was made of crop diversity, wheat and forage crops—grain sorghums, millet, Kafir corn, and broomcorn—soon became the staples of agriculture throughout the Panhandle. For a new county only partially cultivated, Texas County showed surprising results with alfalfa grown in creek bottoms and on some upland soils. Agricultural production and the railroad meant that the days of the old range quickly passed in the county.[8]

A herd law approved by the territorial legislature in 1906 hastened the process. This law required ranchers to fence in their herds to protect farmers' crops. In 1905, Panhandle rancher J. C. Williamson presented the cattlemen's side of the proposed herd law: he asked that cattlemen be granted sufficient time to dispose of their surplus stock without loss. Long and severe winter storms had been hard on range stock; the cattle were thin and needed the benefit of new grass. If the bill under consideration became law, Williamson argued, it would force 100,000 head of range cattle to be sent to market in their worst condition or to be moved to unoccupied free-range lands, which he thought was just as bad. Herding them with countless isolated and unfenced patches of corn and other crops scattered over the plains, he claimed, would be difficult and probably impossible.

Although cattle interests represented "at least 80 percent of the favorable wealth of the county," Williamson said that the cattlemen were willing to give way to settlers. If they could get the benefit of fresh grass, they could come out all right; otherwise many would be ruined. The herd law did force many small-scale ranchers relying on the open range out of business; however, ranchers who owned vast tracts would survive and prosper. For example, by 1921, James K. Hitch owned 12,080 acres in the Panhandle. The herd law and the railroad opened the region to settlers who primarily wished to till the soil.[9]

When the railroad came to Beaver County, Forgan became the shipping center for livestock and produce destined for urban markets. Forgan's commercial activities peaked from 1913 to 1919. People living in Cimarron County were at a disadvantage in getting crops to market and in securing consumer goods until the arrival of a railroad in 1925. Because all the lumber utilized in the county and throughout the Panhandle had to be shipped in, most early settlers gathered cow manure chips to burn for fuel; wood was too valuable to use.[10]

Because no Indians resided in the Panhandle, acquisition of the more than 3 million acres of vacant government land was a relatively easy matter of filing a homestead claim. But when Oklahoma entered the Union, the federal government turned over to the state all public lands, the sale of which was supervised by the school land commissioners. The first sale embraced little more than a million acres, of which 569,613 were allocated to Cimarron County, 182,627 to Texas County, and 195,613 to Beaver County. None of those acres were considered prime agricultural land; it was chiefly used for cattle ranges that, because of the herd law, were considerably under fence. No one could acquire more than 160 acres of agricultural land. However, if less than 37 ½ percent of the land was suitable for farming, it could be denominated as grazing land and sold in tracts not exceeding one section, or 640 acres. Lands having less than 12 ½ percent of tillable surface were classified as mountainous or barren, and these lands, chiefly in Cimarron County, could be sold in tracts not exceeding two sections, or 1,280 acres. Although individuals could not acquire more that 160 acres of agricultural land, each member of one's family could claim this amount. Each purchaser was required to write an affidavit that the land was for their own use and benefit, and they were prohibited from transferring any of their land within five years to anyone else holding as many as 160 acres. The state constitution barred aliens from holding such lands. Residence on the land was not a prerequisite, but the buyer had to establish and maintain lasting improvements, which had to be more than a fence or a crop if the land was classified as grazing land. Landowners had to meet this requirement before securing the title from the state. Such provisions helped to ensure local ownership rather than large corporate ownership of Panhandle lands.[11]

Soon after these lands became available, landowners sought increased water for irrigation purposes. Although well water was plentiful, in many instances these wells were seventy or more feet deep. In 1910, the Northwestern Oklahoma Irrigation Congress met in Guymon and called for government-established pumping stations to demonstrate the practicability and cost of irrigation. In addition, federal funds were requested to help determine whether sites for Reclamation Act projects were feasible in the Panhandle. Water would not be used extensively for irrigation until the 1950s, but where irrigation was used, land and the life surrounding it underwent a vast transformation.[12]

The first report of the State Board of Agriculture for 1907 and 1908 indicated the extent of agricultural development in the Panhandle. In March 1907, Panhandle ranches grazed 25,885 cattle and 14,450 milk cows, a marked decline from the 65,093 cattle recorded in 1906, which was contributable to the herd law. Leading crops were milo/maize (727,017 bushels), Kafir corn (629,286 bushels), wheat (588,255 bushels), and sorghum (21,571 tons for forage). Aside from wheat, the leading crops provided feed for livestock. Distance from large markets and the comparative lack of adequate transportation facilities in many parts of the Panhandle dictated that a large portion of the crops raised be fed to stock.

However, cattlemen had to cope with Texas fever, a contagious cattle disease. The exception was Cimarron County, where the altitude fortified farmers against malaria and herds against Texas fever. Cattle from surrounding states were prohibited from entering the Panhandle, and cattle from the three counties were not allowed to move to any part of Oklahoma before being inspected. All infected cattle and those exposed to them had to be immersed in a dipping vat to remove ticks that spread the disease before being allowed to move to other parts of the state.

Succeeding reports indicate enhanced crop acreage and production. But, as already suggested, production in Texas County mostly surpassed that of its neighbors, and Cimarron County usually lagged behind the other two. Moreover, researchers at Panhandle State College in Goodwell were developing drought-resistant crops, ways to use available water in semi-arid environments, and methods of conserving soil moisture.[13]

In addition, many Panhandle farmers in the Southwest Farmers Congress banded together in 1914 to discuss ways and means of improving production. However, hard rains that lasted for almost four days cancelled a session to discuss dry farming. The Beaver River rose so high it could not be crossed for two days, and the mud was too deep for farmers living close to Guymon to attend. More successful was a meeting during which summer fallowing for wheat was discussed. At other meetings, farmers talked about dairies and creameries, and cantaloupe growers soon involved themselves with the organization.[14]

Texas County got a further boost during these years when a highway paralleling the Rock Island from the Kansas line to Texhoma was constructed. The sixty-six-mile road was opened before 1920 without a single condemnation suit by the county. The road, now Highway 54, saved about one-third of the distance from one town in Texas County to the next one. By 1960, about 2,000 motor vehicles used it every day.[15]

The First World War elevated prices and therefore expanded wheat production. Threshing machines had appeared as early as 1912, and combines and even tractors became evident during the war years. Some farmers realized that the high cost of living made marketing the home-grown food supply profitable as well. Texas County farmer O. N. Heard, for example, explained that his garden always provided an ample supply of vegetables, and he was able to grow some fruit trees as well. Other farmers had equal success with fruits and vegetables. During these years, silos appeared in the Panhandle as the best way to store feed grains and silage. While the rest of the state was suffering from lack of rain in 1918, the Panhandle enjoyed some heavy rains and its farmers emerged from the war years relatively unscathed. This was evident at the Tri-County Fair, held at Guymon in November 1920, where the exhibits showed that the Panhandle was not a one-crop country. A study of those exhibits indicates that the important crops were Kafirs, grain sorghum, broomcorn, and wheat. Visitors were surprised at the various farm products grown. Corn was found among the exhibits, especially those from Cimarron County where the elevation saved it from the hot winds that sometimes engulfed the other two counties.

The production of grain sorghum and Kafir corn as leading crops indicated that the livestock industry would continue to be a significant aspect of the economy, as farmers combined their interests with the stock industry in order to gain wealth and prosperity. The Panhandle in the 1920s reached an apex of productivity never before achieved, with wheat yields leading the way.[16]

Despite the Panhandle's remarkable development and enhanced prosperity, its residents had to live with undependable weather conditions, as did people throughout the High Plains. In 1908 windstorms tore down dozens of windmills in Texas and Cimarron counties. In 1929 tornadoes destroyed houses, barns, fences, and windmills northwest of Texhoma. Blizzards in 1911–1912 and 1918–1919 killed hundreds of cattle. During the great blizzard of 1918–1919, Boise City was cut off from the rest of the region for twenty-one days. A sudden storm with high winds, hail, and a deluge of water did much damage to crops and flooded great strips of the country near Guymon in 1925. A severe hailstorm destroyed crops and property in 1928. A ten-inch rainfall created a lake covering several sections shortly after the railroad came through Gate in 1912. The lake didn't disappear until about 1930.

The worst flood, affecting both the Cimarron and Beaver rivers, occurred in 1914. The rains began on Sunday, April 26, and continued throughout the week. People drowned, wires were downed, and the valleys of both rivers were swept bare of trees, vegetation, and fences. Homes flooded, and farm buildings and property of all kinds were washed away. Livestock drowned and

crops were destroyed. New channels of the Beaver River cut
through some fields and gravel piled up in others. Bridges,
including all but the Rock Island Bridge, washed out. The 1914
flood was the most serious natural disaster to affect the Panhandle prior to the dust storms of the 1930s.[17]

In 1913 a firestorm swept through thirty miles of Texas
County, destroying property in its wake. It burned for two days
before being checked. But, by far, the most unusual storm old-
timers ever witnessed occurred on St. Patrick's Day in 1923. It
came up so quickly that many people were not immediately
aware of its approach. In the north and west materialized "a
great bank of what appeared to be reddish brown and blue-black
clouds, which boiled and rolled and tumbled like the seething
steam and smoke caused by oil fires and explosions." Covering a
large scope of the horizon, it made many people frantic with
fear. For more than an hour in Guymon, intense darkness pre-
vailed. Then, gradually, the light started to appear until finally
the sun began peeping through the dust in fiery red rays.[18] A
frigid wave, ushered in with the wind, caused the temperature to
drop below zero Fahrenheit. Aside from the stifling dust that
penetrated most homes and buildings, the storm did little damage in Guymon. But in the open country, many farm buildings
were damaged and livestock were killed, either by the storm's
fury or the dust. Automobiles were abandoned along the highways, and a number of head-on collisions occurred. The storm
covered a wide scope of territory, causing extensive damage in
eastern Colorado and New Mexico, extending down into Texas,

and traveling as far east as Hutchinson, Kansas, and central Oklahoma. No one living remembered a storm like this one, and they would not see another for a decade.[19]

Yet despite all these impositions, Panhandle farmers, sowing wheat in the fall and sorghum and broomcorn in the spring, harvested their best and biggest crop yields in the 1920s because of a few wet seasons. To bring their wheat into town, farmers near Texhoma tied several wagons together and formed a wagon train. During harvest, the wagons were lined up for half a mile waiting to be loaded. In one year, the town of Knowles in Beaver County shipped 273 freight cars of wheat, 61 cars of other produce, and 14,480 gallons of milk. In Cimarron County, 2 million bushels of high-grade wheat were harvested and shipped out to eastern and northern markets. The crop sold at an average price of $1.13 a bushel. In addition, livestock, poultry, dairy products, corn, and broomcorn shipped in record quantities. For several years in the 1920s, Texas County was the banner wheat county in the nation, and the Panhandle was one of the world's great granaries. At times during the decade, Panhandle wheat won first place in the International Wheat Exposition. In 1928–1929 the town of Hooker in Texas County was considered the most important primary wheat market in the United States. It had seven large elevators into which more than 3 million bushels of wheat were dumped, then passed from chutes into cars destined for eastern milling centers. Crop yields from fifty to seventy-four bushels per acre were recorded in 1926. Acreage increased as more land was cultivated almost every year.

During the 1920s, Panhandle farmers began replacing their former farming equipment, which consisted of horses, harnesses, plows, drills, discs, headers, and threshers. Their purchasing power, in effect, bought the manufacturing plant that produced tractors, combines, discs, plows, and drills of a larger capacity, all of which saved labor and allowed farmers to work larger acreage. Immediately following the wheat harvest in late spring, large gang plows and harrows were hitched behind powerful tractors to cultivate the land. The combine harvesting the wheat distributed straw over the field; the gang plow then plowed it under. As a result, the mammoth straw stacks disappeared. What previously took two to three weeks now could be accomplished in ten days. By this time, most of the big ranches were cut into farms, and the scrub cattle of the range had been replaced with better grades, including dairy herds. Buffalo grass that formerly covered much of the land gave way to the power machinery of prosperous farmers securing record-breaking yields. Yet as of 1927, thousands of acres of virgin soil remained untouched by a plow.[20]

A principle aim of farm operations was to conserve and use the scant rainfall. The land had to be kept in condition to absorb the precipitation, thereby preventing unnecessary moisture loss; in contrast, maintaining soil fertility was primarily important in more humid sections. Summer fallow was profitable only when spring and early summer moisture was so limited that sorghum crops were not likely to make good yields. On many farms, wheat followed wheat year after year, and grain sorghums followed grain sorghums.[21]

The average farm size increased from about 247 acres in
1910 to about 570 in 1930. The census of that year reported that
owners operated more than 60 percent of the farms, and tenants
operated less than 37 percent. Tenancy was increasing because
many producers with small acreages found it profitable to rent
additional land to better use their power machinery. A large
number of tenants were also farm owners. Where they were not,
the land usually was cultivated on a share basis with the tenant
furnishing all equipment and crop expense and delivering one-
third of the crop to the elevator as the landowner's share. In
places of great distance from elevators, the landlord received
only one-fourth of the crop. Cash rent differed according to the
type of land and its distance from town. On some farms, the
operators lived in town or on another farm.[22]

While practically all farms and ranches in the Oklahoma
Panhandle had one or more windmills, oil or gas wells were
almost nonexistent, even though Oklahoma was a leading oil-
producing state. The Texas Panhandle contained a flush field,
bringing profit to landowners and developers, but the Oklahoma
Panhandle at the end of the 1920s had not yielded significant
quantities of oil or gas. Geologists and others continually ex-
plored it, however, hoping to tap a deep pool. Test holes for oil
appeared throughout the three counties by the 1920s. Derricks
to support drills as well as other machinery, arrangements, and
equipment for sinking a hole became obvious. In 1923 the Alli-
son Well No. 1 near Texhoma was designated a gasser estimated
to produce 40 to 50 million feet a day from the 2,635-foot level.

Although this was perhaps the biggest wildcat ever drilled in Oklahoma, technical difficulties intervened; the big gasser broke loose, and nothing came of this venture.[23]

During the rest of the decade work progressed on oil development. Deep holes were dug, and hundreds of individual and company leases were filed with county clerks. Geologists and oilmen scoured potential sites, and in 1925 some talked about drilling test wells that would circle Guymon. By 1928 the Texas County Gas Company provided Guymon fuel for local use, and by the end of the decade the three wells provided Guymon fuel for local use and for customers in all the major towns in Texas County. In the previous year, oil was discovered at 4,095 feet in Cimarron County, but the well was not deep enough to reach the "pay sand."

Geologists were aware of the vast Hugoton Gas Field covering large portions of Texas, Beaver, and surrounding counties in Kansas. Drilling operations occurred at various times. Some wells showed gas, while others were reported dry. In 1929 two gas wells near Guymon yielded respectively 15 million and 8 million cubic feet of gas per day to serve customers in that community. By 1930 about fourteen wells had been located or drilled in Texas County; eight wells had been drilled in Cimarron County without production. Texas County received more "play" than all the rest of the Oklahoma Panhandle, but no major strikes occurred.[24]

In the two decades following statehood, a prosperous and productive Oklahoma Panhandle grew from a pioneering region

in which people lived in sod houses and dugouts to one that supported a renowned granary and grazing lands. Like the Australian Outback, the Panhandle was still sparsely populated, but
its remarkable development during so brief a period made it
exceptional among neighboring areas that developed their
economies over a much longer period and were not nearly as isolated from their respective states as the three Panhandle counties.
The rapid development had interesting side effects. For example,
Caucasians inhabited the region almost exclusively; Indians,
African Americans, and Hispanics were rarely evident. And as the
size of farms and ranches increased, the population decreased
slightly: in 1907 the three counties had a combined population of
35,739; in 1930 this figure stood at 30,960. Increasingly mechanized agriculture required fewer farm hands, horses, and mules,
thereby contributing to the declining population. As always, Texas
County ranked first, trailed closely by Beaver County, with
Cimarron County being a distant third. This ranking, incidentally, held for almost every set of data pertaining to the economic
development of the Oklahoma Panhandle.[25]

As the 1920s came to an end, Panhandle residents had every
reason to believe their good times would continue. Like all farming areas, they had dealt with floods, fires, drought, blizzards,
and severe winds. They had taken those adversities in stride and
quickly overcome them. However, the coming decade would try
them in ways no one could have imagined.

The Oklahoma Panhandle in the

1930s and 1940s

In its biennial report for 1929–1930, the Oklahoma State Board of Agriculture reported that "no greater progress has been made in agriculture during any two year period since statehood." However that was not the case in Beaver, Texas, and Cimarron counties, where wheat sown in dry soil failed to germinate and some replanting was necessary. In 1931 adequate rainfall allowed farmers once again to produce bumper crops of wheat, corn, and grain sorghum, only to face a collapsing national economy. Prices plummeted to a point where many Panhandle farmers could not recover the cost of harvesting. Ranchers faced a similarly disastrous fall in prices. Conditions were comparable throughout the Southern Great Plains. Whatever degree of prosperity the Oklahoma Panhandle had enjoyed in the 1920s disappeared as the Great Depression threatened the profitable economic base enjoyed by its residents.[1]

Whether the Dust Bowl was a horrendous, man-made ecological disaster predicated on a capitalist system driven by a rampant search for profits or an extreme manifestation of a natural occurrence that had a long history of affecting life on the Plains is an argument almost unending among interested parties, and it is central to this chapter's concern with land use—how residents used the resources available to them, how they coped with crisis, and what they learned.[2]

Settlers in Cimarron, Texas, and Beaver counties at statehood (1907) and earlier found a barren grass country, high and flat with scant rainfall and continuous winds that at times bordered on hurricane force. In spite of the challenges, they cultivated the land, and for about a quarter of a century, despite occasional drought and one notable dust storm in 1923, the Panhandle prospered. This situation changed in the 1930s, despite the fact that the soils were naturally fertile in most places. The soil developed under a grass cover assisted by comparatively low rainfall. The grass cover added nitrogen as well as organic matter to the soil. The low annual rainfall also allowed little leaching of plant-food elements to occur, and this helped maintain natural fertility.

Moisture was always the limiting factor in crop production. The low rainfall made it imperative to utilize the precipitation efficiently. That was accomplished with crops adapted to the prevailing sub-humid conditions and by preventing unnecessary moisture loss. These were the essential keys to grappling with farming in the Panhandle. More farmers pursued efficient use of precipitation in the 1930s, which became the essence of the New Deal programs devoted to agriculture as well. The leading proponent who helped spread the message throughout the Panhandle and later throughout the Southern Great Plains was a long-time professor at the Panhandle Agricultural and Mechanical College (A&M) in Goodwell, H. H. Finnell.[3]

While depression continued throughout most of the decade, it was merely the first of the three "D"s that afflicted the region. Adequate rainfall abruptly ended late in 1931. Drought, combined with hot winds and the lack of moisture, ensured a marked decline in crop production. And soon the third "D," dust, firmly established itself through awesome storms that made life miserable, and at times unbearable, for both humans and livestock. However, by the end of the 1930s conditions improved significantly, and prosperity returned during World War II. At war's end the three counties comprising the Oklahoma Panhandle were on the verge of developments that would ensure even greater prosperity and make a repetition of the three "D"s a remote possibility.

Beginning in May 1933, two years after the drought started, dust storms wreaked havoc across the Southern Great Plains for several years. In the Oklahoma Panhandle the storms reached blizzard proportions, notably in May 1934, April 1935, and April 1937. Whether it was a blizzard, a dirty haze, or a sand storm, blowing dirt made life miserable for all living things. For example, on a comparatively clear day in May 1935, the town of Beaver and outlying territory were engulfed in a dust storm that left the area in utter darkness for two hours. The storms finally abated over the Southern Great Plains by the fall of 1938.[4]

Row crops were burning up by the fall of 1933, though fortunately a good wheat crop was harvested in the late spring despite low prices. Feed was scarce, and stock was beginning to shrink. Some farmers ran livestock on their wheat pastures. Others turned back to horses in row-crop sections. Always there was hope of rain. When it came, fields turned green only to wither shortly thereafter. Not much wheat went to the market. Instead of coal, families burnt prairie coal (dry cattle dung).[5]

The Cimarron County attorney succinctly explained what was occurring in a letter to Senator Elmer Thomas:

> The citizenship of the panhandle have at times been self sus-taining and have never, heretofore, requested help. The situa-tion at this time however is one too large to cope with, the high winds and continued drouth has left our lands in a horrible condition. Not one acre of wheat will be harvested . . . and the cattle due to lack of food have not as yet shed their winter coat of hair. In fact our county is a barren waste, our county funds are exhausted and we have a number of destitute families, and that number will increase rapidly during the year. There was quite a number of R.F.C. [Reconstruction Finance Corpora-tion] loans secured, which helped materially but the crops planted with the funds have been blown out, and in the event we do not receive rain within the next twenty days, our hopes for a row crop are nil . . . Large numbers of cattle have been shipped to other counties, and without assistance, the class of citizenship we have, even though hardy, honest, and used to hardships, are going to be compelled to leave. We are not asking for charity, the people are just not able to meet the prevailing conditions.[6]

On June 16, 1933, in Guymon at the approximate center of the Oklahoma Panhandle and the seat of Texas County, officials of the town's Red Cross and Chamber of Commerce convened a meeting to discuss the distress caused by depression and

Working on the Beaver Railroad, circa 1903. Courtesy Western History Collections, University of Oklahoma Libraries. Reprinted with permission.

Freighters arriving in Beaver, Oklahoma, from Liberal, Kansas, circa 1904. Courtesy Western History Collections, University of Oklahoma Libraries. Reprinted with permission.

A field of grain sorghum (often called milo or maize) in the Oklahoma Panhandle circa 1909. Grain sorghum is the chief food crop raised in the Panhandle. Courtesy Western History Collections, University of Oklahoma Libraries. Reprinted with permission.

Wheat Field Near Guymon Okla. 09'

Harvesting wheat near Guymon, Oklahoma, 1909. Courtesy Western History Collections, University of Oklahoma Libraries. Reprinted with permission.

Meandering of the Cimarron River from the top of Black Mesa, two miles north of Kenton and the highest point in Oklahoma, July 20, 1916. Courtesy Western History Collections, University of Oklahoma Libraries. Reprinted with permission.

Boise City, seat of Cimarron County, 1916. Courtesy Western History Collections, University of Oklahoma Libraries. Reprinted with permission.

*Stacking hay on the O.W. Tucker Ranch, 1924. Courtesy Western History
Collections, University of Oklahoma Libraries.
Reprinted with permission.*

Sheep herd and cows on the O.W. Tucker Ranch, 1929. Courtesy Western History Collections, University of Oklahoma Libraries. Reprinted with permission.

Grain sorghum harvest on the O.W. Tucker Ranch, near Kenton, in Cimarron County, 1924. Courtesy Western History Collections, University of Oklahoma Libraries. Reprinted with permission.

O.W. Tucker and John Freeman making hay on the Tucker ranch, 1929. Courtesy Western History Collections, University of Oklahoma Libraries. Reprinted with permission.

Cattle that perished during the 1930s drought were purchased and then disposed of by agents of the Agricultural Adjustment Administration. Courtesy Western History Collections, University of Oklahoma Libraries.
Reprinted with permission.

*Dust storm approaching
downtown Guymon, June
1937. Courtesy Western
History Collections,
University of Oklahoma
Libraries.
Reprinted with permission.*

C.W. Tucker and his son Kenton discussing with Hugh Bennett (CENTER), *chief of the Soil Conservation Service, the alfalfa harvest, Cimarron County, September, 11, 1940. This alfalfa field was irrigated by water shared in a reservoir made possible through the Water Facilities Program of the Soil Conservation Service. Courtesy Western History Collections, University of Oklahoma Libraries. Reprinted with permission.*

Panhandle wheat harvest, circa 1945. Thanks to abundant rainfall, the Dust Bowl era was becoming a faded memory. Courtesy Western History Collections, University of Oklahoma Libraries. Reprinted with permission.

LEFT *Crawford Number 1—the first gas well drilled in the Hugoton Field. Courtesy Stevens County Gas and Historical Museum, Hugoton, Kansas. Reprinted with permission.* RIGHT *Drilling for water on the Layton farm, November 1952. Layton's rig had already reached a depth of ninety-one feet. Courtesy Western History Collections, University of Oklahoma Libraries. Reprinted with permission.*

A Kuhn Bros. spudder rig used to dig the hole over which the drilling rig was then moved. Courtesy Stevens County Gas and Historical Museum, Hugoton, Kansas. Reprinted with permission.

Steam rig boilers used to generate a power supply. Courtesy Stevens County Gas and Historical Museum, Hugoton, Kansas. Reprinted with permission.

Well blowing after acidizing. Courtesy Stevens County Gas and Historical Museum, Hugoton, Kansas. Reprinted with permission.

*A drilling rig. Courtesy Stevens
County Gas and Historical
Museum, Hugoton, Kansas.
Reprinted with permission.*

*Aerial photograph of U.S. Bureau of Mines Helium Plant at Keyes, Cimarron
County, 1964. Helium is extracted only from natural gas. This plant, which began
production in 1959, is no longer operative. Courtesy of Oklahoma Department of
Commerce. Reprinted with permission.*

*Aerial view of Seaboard Farms, circa 1997. Courtesy
Seaboard Farms, Inc. Reprinted with permission.*

*Entrance to Seaboard Farms, Guymon, Oklahoma. Courtesy Seaboard Farms, Inc.
Reprinted with permission.*

Hogs in holding pens at Seaboard Farms processing plant in Texas County. From the Sunday Oklahoman, May 18, 1997; photograph by David McDaniel. Copyright © 1997, the Oklahoma Publishing Company. Reprinted with permission.

Hog-barn operators at Seaboard Farms pump hog waste into lagoons averaging one to two acres. Most hold ten to twenty thousand gallons of wastewater. From the Sunday Oklahoma, May 4, 1997; photograph by David McDaniel. Copyright © 1997, the Oklahoma Publishing Company. Reprinted with permission.

drought and to seek federal assistance. It attracted a large crowd of concerned citizens, along with representatives of the governors of Oklahoma, Texas, Kansas, and New Mexico. What the audience heard was an extended tale of woe: cattle dying, almost no wheat in areas that previously harvested 4 to 6 million bushels, 90 percent of the poultry dead in one Panhandle county because of sand storms, milk cows turned onto the highways to starve, and much more. Reports of the meeting went to the area's representatives in Washington requesting assistance from the emerging New Deal.[7] In addition, R. F. Baker of Hooker said that at least forty destructive windstorms had already swept the Oklahoma Panhandle in 1933.[8]

Was this a temporary calamity or something more serious? Residents of the Panhandle disagreed among themselves, and some left for California, Oregon, or nearby towns and cities. It was estimated that approximately 40 percent of Panhandle farm families moved but not necessarily out of state. Most residents stuck it out, hoping if not praying for rain, taking advantage of New Deal programs, and all the while modifying their agricultural practices to utilize the land more efficiently by conserving the soil.

While high winds were nothing new to Panhandle residents, the winds soon carried away soil from plowed lands and piled it in mounds on highways, along fences, and around buildings. Fields never touched by plows were swept clean down to the hard dirt. Two years of drought, a Red Cross county chairman explained, "has made our people penniless and unless conditions change, they will need [to] be helped until they can get on their feet, or until we raise a wheat crop here."[9]

Deplorable as conditions were in 1933, they would get worse when the vegetation cover disappeared from sandy soils. Peak winds, up to thirty miles an hour, caused serious erosion with high sand drifts filling yards and covering farm implements, tanks, troughs, woodpiles, shrubs, and young trees. Sand drifts piled along fence rows, across roads, and around Russian thistles and other plants. But already a handful of specialists suggested ways and means of reclaiming wind-swept soils. H. H. Finnell, director of the experiment station at Panhandle A&M College, claimed that soil could be rebuilt to a productive state. But the more immediate problem was reclaiming dust-covered soils. Farmers noticed that fields covered with trash (crop residues) collected dust and prevented removal of the soil. Thus Finnell's message essentially was to cover the land and to engage in practices that would keep available moisture in the soil, allowing soil bacteria to thrive. He suggested that contour listing would bring up deep soil to mix with the dust accumulation and thus encourage the necessary bacterial activity. Terracing would also make it possible to increase soil moisture and support vegetative growth.

To prevent soil blowing, Finnell and others insisted that farmers keep crop residue or clods on the surface. Growing vegetables between strips of sorghum or corn also prevented soil blowing. Farming in large blocks allowed soil drift to spread quickly from one field to another, but for reasonably sized holdings, Finnell and other specialists claimed that soil blowing could

be controlled by proper management of crop cover and cultivation. Though rain was of more immediate concern to Panhandle
farmers, Finnell's message and that of his colleagues did not go
unheard. Increasing numbers of farmers took heed and modified
their practices. Few lost faith in the future because they knew
what the land could produce, despite the fact that they were living through the worst general drought ever experienced in the
United States.[10]

The drought, the dust storms, and the Depression wrought
significant changes in the demography of the Panhandle. While
the percentage of farms operated by tenants in 1935 never
reached above 40 percent, the foreclosure record is more revealing. As of February 1934, total foreclosed acreage stood at
8,039.12 acres in Beaver County, at 1,680 acres in Cimarron
County, and at 2,120.80 acres in Texas County. By June 1935,
the figure in Texas County jumped to 3,400.80 acres. As of April
1935, the Oklahoma Emergency Relief Administration indicated
a caseload of 1,157, or 42.43 percent of the population, for
Beaver County; of 361, or 28.03 percent, for Cimarron County;
and 722, or 21.50 percent, for Texas County. In the five years
from 1930 to 1935 the population shifted from 11,452 to 7,836
in Beaver County, from 5,408 to 3,109 in Cimarron County, and
from 14,100 to 7,065 in Texas County.[11]

When it rained, as it occasionally did in different places and
at different times, farmers placed greater emphasis on forage
and feed crops. Such a change in land use necessitated an
increase in the size of farms. More than 111,000 cattle ranged

the Panhandle counties in 1935. Without an improvement in the weather, the area would have reverted more heavily to a livestock economy with larger ranches and fewer people. Thanks to the work of Finnell and others, along with the efforts of agents of the Soil Conservation Service (SCS) established by Congress in 1935, the battle to protect crops against the wind began in earnest. Yet a handful of farmers managed for themselves. When his fields began to blow, Mrs. Ray Oakley's father used his one-horse lister to plow deep enough to make ridges in the fields so that the wind would not pick up the soil. During the years of drought, she recalled her father realizing from four to nine bushels of wheat per acre.[12]

The RFC, through its Regional Agricultural Credit Corporations, loaned money to farmers and ranchers before it was replaced by the Production Credit associations, created in 1933. Those agencies were among many that established offices in the Panhandle. They were joined by technicians, engineers, agronomists, chemists, soil surveyors, and others, who all, in one way or another, helped to attack the wasting of land. However, Paul Bonnifield, a Dust Bowl scholar examining Texas and Cimarron counties, played down the role of government in fighting the drought and depression, calling it merely "useful." He admired the fortitude and resourcefulness of the people who "found ways of surviving and maintaining the vital aspects of their community."[13]

New Deal agencies offered aid at the outset. The Federal Emergency Relief Administration (FERA) provided families with assistance, the Civil Works Administration (CWA) put men to work leveling sand dunes and cleaning roads, seed loans were available, and farmers signed up for programs calling for crop reduction even though few farmers produced meaningful crops. The Agricultural Adjustment Association (AAA) paid farmers to curtail their planting of wheat. Other programs furnished crop and feed subsistence loans. After 1935 the Works Progress Administration (WPA) provided jobs to further the work of rehabilitating the land.

In May 1935, the extension service of Oklahoma A&M College in Stillwater conducted a series of meetings throughout the Panhandle. The meeting in Beaver was attended by about 800 farmers, about 40 percent of the total number of farmers in the county. A similar meeting in Boise City attracted more than 400 farmers, about half the farmers in Cimarron County. Six hundred farmers attended the meeting at Goodwell, also about half the farmers in Texas County. At those meetings officials announced a program to combat wind erosion through contour listing and other techniques. Farmers agreeing to participate would not pay taxes on gasoline, which they purchased at about eight cents a gallon, and they would receive a fuel allotment, all in a massive effort to reestablish a protective covering on the land. With the help of committees of farmers and landowners, each county agent directed the programs. The services of governmental agencies were provided without charge to all participants. In return, farmers who used their own implements agreed to follow practices suggested by the county committee.[14]

Caroline Henderson, a Panhandle resident since 1906, found ways of surviving but valued what the New Deal was seeking to accomplish. She and her husband held a quarter-section homestead near Eva in Texas County, which they worked together until the late 1950s. In 1935 she wrote to Secretary of Agriculture Henry A. Wallace, detailing the recent history of the Panhandle through her experiences. She gave credit, "next to the enduring character of our people," to the "various activities of the federal government," whose assistance provided for "the continued occupation of the plains country" and ensured that large sections of it were not "virtually abandoned." She recognized, as did Bonnifield and others, that "life goes on in a manner surprisingly near to normal." All the same she understood that this was possible "through the rental checks under the wheat acreage control program," though, like other farmers, she was not enthusiastic about voluntarily restricting production. Nevertheless, she regarded the control programs as an enormous benefit and "a definite means of continuing decent home life and the effort at least toward productive labor." She admired the flexibility of the AAA and its Panhandle agents in adapting "to new or unforeseen conditions." And she was not alone in stating, "In our own part of the country the voluntary response to the campaign for controlled production as an experiment for the benefit of farmers was practically unanimous."

In addition, Henderson noted that in Texas County, the CWA and FERA reportedly had spent a total of $331,170.69. That money, she remarked, helped clear and improve roads, cut down sand hills, fill in eroded valleys, and construct reservoirs. "The crooked has been made straight" and "the rough places plain." Such efforts, besides improving the land, provided jobs and hope to desperate farmers, gave them a voice in determining aspects of the agricultural programs, and allowed family life in the Panhandle counties to maintain its essential dignity and people to pursue their daily endeavors without restriction. Government agencies supplemented peoples' efforts to preserve their land and livestock, "and in various ways showing interest in our struggles for existence" until some happier day when problems that no one could solve individually would abate.[15]

In letters to a friend, Henderson vividly elaborated on the conditions in her part of the Dust Bowl. She related how they had to ship their cattle to grass outside of the Panhandle. She also noted that within a few weeks in June 1935, 299,986 acres had been plowed or listed in contour lines by farmers anxious to take advantage of the federal government's offer of ten cents per acre toward the expense of fuel and oil for tractors or feed for horses. They understood the necessity for distributing moisture evenly over fields and lessening the impact of wind erosion. She noted too that official reports emphasized the eagerness with which people accepted "any sort of work to help themselves and to make unnecessary the acceptance of public aid." Further helping to meliorate conditions a 1935 Oklahoma law permitted county commissioners to require the working of land hitherto allowed to blow, a law that she said was already operative in Texas County.

Henderson was impressed with the planting methods encouraged by the SCS, which called for "listing on contour lines and laying up terraces to check the run-off in whatever rains might come." Like many of her neighbors, she was distressed and even embittered "over the recent AAA decision in the Supreme Court" because the AAA benefit payments and wages from federal work projects were "all that have saved a large territory here from abandonment." She was further distressed "by the extent to which land once owned and occupied by farm families is now passing into ownership of banks, mortgage companies, assurance societies, and investment partnerships or corporations." She reported notices of foreclosure proceedings and of sheriffs' sales in "our county paper" involving the ownership of 3,520 acres of land.

While land ownership changed, Henderson sensed a general spirit of optimism furthered by forward-looking government undertakings, including "erosion control experiments scattered over a wide area." Moreover, the WPA was employing men to survey contour lines, lay up terraces, remove drifted soil from fence rows, fill gullies, cut down dead trees and dig holes for resetting trees in favorable locations, and reseed wind-blown spaces. All of that and more was done without expense to farmers who agreed to cooperate and participate in individual conferences to develop programs to suit their farms. In short, though dust storms were a frequent occurrence and the drought had not abated, thanks to the functioning of New Deal programs, life in the Oklahoma Panhandle by the end of 1935 and into 1936 was not as bleak as it had been and prospects for further improvement were enhanced every time it rained. Farmers and ranchers were learning how to cope with the Dust Bowl.[16]

By 1936 the government emphasized improved land use. It offered Panhandle farmers ten cents per acre for contour listing on shifting acres. In Texas County, 305,257 acres were contour-listed. In addition nearly 6,000 acres were terraced. In all, 622 farms were worked to control erosion. In neighboring Beaver County, 191,000 acres were contracted for contouring, and 4,000 acres were terraced. Engineering crews worked long hours running contour lines under disagreeable circumstances until federal funding ran out. Those farms then were better able to stop erosion. When rains came during the late spring and summer, water was held in place where it fell. For the first time in several years, scanty rainfall allowed crop production in some parts of the Panhandle. In 1935 wheat was making eight to ten bushels an acre. Thereafter, with improved moisture conditions, a bigger wheat acreage was anticipated. Subsumed in the exuberance about improved conditions was the question of whether a closer correlation existed between properly handled soils and grain production or between rainfall and grain production. Was conserving soil more important than conserving moisture?[17]

The work of the United States Department of Agriculture (USDA) in the Panhandle was directed, as was the message of Finnell and others, toward putting a vegetative cover on the soil and providing protection by means of crop residues, stalks, and stubble when no crop occupied the land. By 1935 that message was having an impact with increasing frequency. Ranchers also more frequently controlled grazing and created contoured furrows on gently sloping range lands to prevent runoff. Livestock watering places were developed, and the federal government rescued dying cattle.

One of the most remarkable developments during those years came as the result of private initiative. Cimarron County residents had long talked of a small dam on the Cimarron River, but previous attempts to dam the stream had always washed out. In 1933 Julius Kohler designed a dam and with his son's help constructed a 300-foot, steel-reinforced dam that furnished irrigation for 700 acres of valley land, a marked contrast to the surrounding eroded countryside. Within four years Kohler had paid off the loan for constructing a dam that enabled him to prosper during those troubled times despite the lack of adequate rainfall.[18]

Prior to the 1930s rainfall usually averaged between fifteen and nineteen inches annually with most of the precipitation, about 75 percent, falling during the spring and summer. But from 1932 to 1937 rainfall was about five or six inches less than in previous years. The full fury of the drought descended in 1933, and large sections of the Panhandle became arid and desert-like and remained so until late in the decade. Recovery was slow and sporadic. But the point to be noted is that by late 1935 and 1936 increasing numbers of Panhandle residents had worked their way out of the ordeal nature had imposed upon them. Nevertheless, three little words, "if it rains," ruled life in the Dust Bowl. By 1938 rain fell a bit more frequently.[19]

In 1937 a government-sponsored, range conservation program was launched. Grazing capacity established by a county committee would determine the number of animals the range could carry on a twelve-month basis without injury to forage or watershed. If ranchers agreed to withhold 25 percent of their land from grazing for six months, they would receive an allowance amounting to fifty cents per head of cattle. Similarly, they would receive funding for contour listing, ridging, and terracing; construction of earthen tanks, fences, and fireguards; rodent eradication; destruction of prickly pears; and otherwise improving and rescuing their land from infestations. Participation was voluntary; local committees would evaluate the parameters of compliance with guidelines developed as part of the USDA program.[20]

The success of those efforts was soon evident. Before and after photographs published in the *Oklahoma Farmer-Stockman* told the story—before: abandoned fields; two years later: a sorghum crop on the same field that sold for seven dollars an acre; before: runoff from rainfall that formed a shallow lake; after: contour listing holding water from a similar rain. Another photograph showed deep furrows that held blowing sand. The pictures and the stories indicated that with cooperation, erosion could be seriously reduced and crop production increased. Examples of profitable crops were noted with greater frequency beginning in 1937. Farmers were harvesting more wheat than in the previous six years. And at the western end of the Panhandle the largest privately owned, man-made irrigation lake in Oklahoma produced alfalfa, a crop requiring plenty of moisture, to feed livestock on the 3,200-acre O. W. Tucker ranch. With the assistance of the SCS, the Farm Security Administration, the Cimarron County agent, and engineers from the extension service, Tucker's irrigated acreage also produced melons, peaches, beans, and other crops to supplement his ranching program. County agent William E. Baker summed it all up when he said, "Cover-crops and good management have worked out salvation."[21]

As the following figures for bushels of wheat produced indicate, crop production in the Panhandle markedly increased at the end of the decade.[22]

	1935	1937	1939	1940
Beaver	148,000	703,900	1,474,800	3,207,000
Cimarron	—	—	454,900	812,000
Texas	451,300	831,000	1,345,800	2,315,000

In brief, by the end of the decade, with rainfall at times reaching near-normal levels, crop production in the Panhandle was coming back to previous levels. The Dust Bowl, with about one million Panhandle acres protected from wind erosion, was diminishing.

As the three counties emerged from the 1930s, demographic changes were evident. As in earlier decades, the number of farms declined, while their average size increased. The following chart indicates that farm ownership was also changing.

	Number of Farms		Average Size		Farm Ownership					
					Full		Part		Tenants	
	1930	1940	1930	1940	1930	1940	1930	1940	1930	1940
Beaver	2,047	1,659	511	651	676	451	726	564	627	637
Cimarron	887	605	1,203	1,563	219	110	353	233	308	258
Texas	2,020	1,408	570	820	564	307	694	480	750	616

Declension was evident with regard to population. In 1930 a total of 30,970 people lived in the three Panhandle counties. By 1940 the figure was down to 22,198.[23]

By the latter part of the 1930s the SCS played a key role in working with farmers to improve their land use. But when it came to the formation of soil conservation districts, sentiments were divided. After extensive debate a district was established in Beaver County in 1940.

Fortunately, the minutes of the meeting in Beaver County are available and provide some indication of the concerns of Panhandle farmers and ranchers. The meeting in the community hall in Beaver was prompted by a petition signed by 828 farmers requesting a hearing to determine the feasibility of organizing a soil conservation district. On the part of some in attendance, there were indications of hostility toward "white collars" offering plans that would get "our heads in a halter." That argument was quickly refuted when it became clear that no plan would be adopted unless a majority approved.

As for individual farms, the planning of a program would cost the farmer nothing and he would have the option of accepting or rejecting it. Moreover, if labor was available from Civilian Conservation Corps camps (there were none in the Panhandle), help would be provided, but farmers would have to assist whenever possible, for example, in constructing ponds, developing or improving drainage work, and treating critical slopes and badly eroded lands. Some farmers opposed the proposal "to avoid dictatorship"; others favored the creation of a district because they no longer possessed adequate and ample farm equipment to restore their land fully. But one point was made clear: no "white collars" were going to force anything on any farmer. Agency experts were on hand to assist farmers by making them aware of new ways and means of improving land use.

Some people in the audience pointed out that by utilizing soil conservation techniques they had raised crops where none grew previously. There were even words of support for "white collars" by those who followed their suggestions to gain a larger yield and a better price for their products. Some farmers who hesitated said they already were engaged in practices that conserved soil and moisture. But most of the 216 farmers at the meeting recognized the voluntary aspects of the program and supported the creation of the Beaver County Soil Conservation District.[24] In Cimarron County a similar proposal was decisively defeated in 1945 by a vote of 287 to 82. Texas County never considered the matter. Nevertheless, in the post–World War II years all three counties had well-established soil conservation districts.

By 1939 and 1940 it was already clear to most residents and many observers that the Panhandle was not a "Desert on the March." Farmers who cared for their land and kept it from blowing by listing and planting row crops when wheat failed were harvesting yields that rivaled those in the previous decade. While no one could say bumper crops and prosperity had returned to stay, neither could they say that the Oklahoma Panhandle was a permanent dust bowl. And the productivity of the Panhandle during the 1940s led many to conclude that prosperity truly was there to stay.

During the war years most of the Panhandle enjoyed above average rainfall, and crops brought favorable prices. Wind erosion control was practically built-in because abundant crops left protective residue on the land. And abundant crops, along with good returns, prompted Texas County in 1940 to hold its first county fair in eight years. It illustrated the transition taking place from single-crop farming to a more balanced agriculture and announced that the Panhandle was emerging from years of crises. Officials hoped to expand the fair to include all three counties in 1941.[25]

Two Japanese families from internment camps in California helped to increase production on the farm of Julius Kohler, whose dam on the Cimarron River provided water for irrigation throughout the 1930s. They farmed 160 acres profitably. But for farms without the benefit of a permanent irrigation dam, larger farms meant sounder agriculture. The percentage of farms over 380 acres in the Panhandle increased from 49 percent in 1935 to 61.7

percent in 1940. And by 1943, 58 percent of Panhandle farms utilized hired labor. The military draft kept the figure high.[26]

An example of changes in Panhandle practices was featured in a story about the 2-Bar Ranch of Otto Barby and sons in Beaver County. The ranch annually maintained about 2,000 cows for breeding purposes and grazed about 40,000 acres of land. The Barbys carefully cared for their ranges and protected the short grass—buffalo and the gramas—by the practice of deferred grazing, in some places for two years, and by alternating pastures. On most of their ranges, livestock did not have to go more than a half mile for water from one of the many ponds, wells, or springs on the ranch. Overgrazing was avoided by "one animal unit" per fifteen to seventeen acres to protect the range.

Otto Barby paid high tribute to the government range program for its efforts in protecting the land. In addition, the Barbys carefully maintained a few thousand acres of plow land. By October, their ranch, like most of the Oklahoma Panhandle, was a checkerboard of green and red-brown, with the neutral tones of dry grass serving to soften the contrast between verdant fields of wheat and the maroon of ripening grain sorghum. Meanwhile, thousands of cattle and sheep were turning wheat pasture into meat and wool. When the wheat fields were covered with snow, the sorghums would carry the animals along. Abundant grass, crops, and livestock, thanks to the wet weather, were the trio that sustained prosperity in the Panhandle during the 1940s. There was convincing evidence that farmers and ranchers had learned how to work with nature in the process of restoration.[27]

By 1944 Panhandle farmers talked about the "best crop since '26." Then, however, there was a much larger acreage and therefore a larger yield. At that time "50-bushel wheat and fat cattle" were evident "within rifle shot of some 'deserted village' pictures chosen by government agencies only a few years ago." At a farmers' forum in 1945, those in attendance recognized that droughts would come and winds would blow again, but they did not envision another dust bowl. All agreed with Cimarron County agent William E. Baker, who said, "We can avert another dust bowl if we cling to what experience has taught us—to keep part of the land in grass and a protective cover on the crop land which has a tendency to blow."[28]

Panhandle farmers and ranchers turned in increasing numbers to sorghums as a means of rehabilitating the soil. In the 1930s farmers learned of the ability of this desert-born crop to withstand drought, to anchor the soil against devastating winds, and to provide protection for re-seeded perennial grasses. Without that hardy and versatile plant, the process of re-vegetation with grass would have been seriously retarded. Sorghums had fed poultry and livestock when grass failed to grow and wheat fields blew away. In its various forms, including milo and Kafir, grain sorghums, while not replacing wheat, emerged as the second most important crop produced in the Oklahoma Panhandle. In addition, alfalfa appeared as a major feed crop. The crop raised on the Henry C. Hitch ranch in 1949 became a show piece and prompted an increase in its production throughout the Panhandle.[29]

In *Oklahoma Foot-Loose and Fancy-Free* (1949), Angie Debo commented on the prosperity of the Panhandle. In the summer of 1948 a traveler noted more than one hundred combines "moving along on less than 50 miles of highway." These machines assisted farmers in harvesting their crops. Railroad cars were involved in "a two-way shuttle" with loaded trains pulling out and empties going in. Nevertheless, the system clogged, elevators quickly filled, and trucks waited. Many farmers poured their wheat on the ground to await processing. The greatest harvest, that of 1947, saw "seven and one half million bushels at one time piled in the fields," according to the three county agents' best estimate. The Oklahoma Panhandle once again was a leading granary, one of the nation's great wheat-producing areas.[30]

Prosperity meant that a handful of farmers installed irrigation systems. Nearly all farm, industrial, and town supplies of water were obtained through wells. And nearly every farm utilized a windmill to pump water for livestock. Prosperity also meant that more farmers received electricity from Rural Electric Authority cooperatives and private power companies. With the extension of electricity came many new home and farm appliances, and new farm-to-market roads appeared. With evidence of abundance and well-being easily observed, the Panhandle at the end of the decade was poised for even greater prosperity.[31]

While geologists and others knew of the existence of the vast Ogallala Aquifer, the technology to utilize its waters for irrigation was not easily available, and its properties and dimensions were not fully understood. Wells drilled almost anywhere in the three counties provided an abundant supply of good water for domestic and stock use as well as for municipal, industrial, and railroad purposes. Generally they were more than 100 feet deep. Equipped with windmills, they were capable of pumping a few gallons of water per minute; some were equipped with pump jacks for operation with small gasoline engines when the wind was inadequate.

The Dust Bowl years prompted interest in the possibility of irrigation with water pumped from deep wells. It was hoped that the gas field in the central part of Texas County would furnish fuel at a cost low enough to offset the expense of high pumping lifts. In the 1940s gas was not available to most farmers, though a few irrigation wells were in use. The depth to water in the Panhandle ranged from less than 50 feet to about 300 feet below the surface. Drilled wells had to be cased all the way to the bottom and deep well pumps used. An irrigation well at Panhandle A&M College yielded 960 gallons per minute. Given the various uses of water already mentioned, the total pumpage was small, probably not exceeding 2 million gallons per day. The depth of the water and the cost of power for pumping limited irrigation possibilities to favored areas possessing low pumping lifts or low power rates in combination with other desirable features, such as level land and good soils. Thus, by the end of the 1940s, the existence of the Ogallala formation undergirding 70,000 square miles of Southern High Plains and the huge natural gas field were known, but the technology to exploit those vast resources fully would not be fully realized until the following decade.[32]

The most promising development was the Hugoton Gas Field sprawling beneath sections of Kansas, Oklahoma, and Texas like a giant boot. Guymon was located almost in the exact center of the field. Experts claimed it contained trillions of cubic feet of natural gas. By 1948 wells in the Guymon area had been producing 40 million cubic feet of gas daily for several decades, enough to meet local needs. Cities Service, Phillips Petroleum Company, Skelly Oil Company, and Republic Natural Gas Company then stepped up their activities. In Cimarron County the Price Oil Company opened a new gas field with one well producing a gas flow estimated at 19 million cubic feet per day in 1943. Test wells had been drilled there as well in the late 1920s. The Gulf Oil Corporation also pursued oil and gas possibilities in the county.[33]

Development of natural gas strengthened the hope that fuel for pumping water soon would be available at a cost low enough to overcome the obvious disadvantage of high pumping lifts and to make large-scale irrigation feasible. In 1948 Robert Buster introduced "sprinkling irrigation" on his farm south of Guymon. His success raised the possibility that the Oklahoma Panhandle could achieve economic stability, thereby ensuring that its prosperity would not be an evanescent occurrence dependent upon climatic conditions.[34]

Entering the second half of the twentieth century the three Panhandle counties boasted a combined population of 26,135, up from the 1940 population of 22,200 but still falling short of the 30,900 in 1930. More revealing, however, was the decline of the rural farm population to 10,369 in 1950 from 13,246 in 1940. Rural population declined as farming operations expanded. The per capita income in 1950 came to $1,535 for Beaver County, $1,626 for Cimarron County, and $1,375 for Texas County. Those figures surpassed the state average of $1,127 and were exceeded by only three counties: Tulsa, Oklahoma, and Washington, home of the Phillips Petroleum Company. In addition, by 1955 there were 41,300 irrigated acres (32,000 in Texas County) in the Panhandle, and more than 3.4 million acres were operated by 3,246 farmer-ranchers in 1950. Those impressive figures suggested that residents in the Oklahoma Panhandle could look forward to a more prosperous future. They had moved in two decades from depression, drought, and dust to prosperity based on improved land use and favorable climatic conditions.[35]

Optima Dam

A Failed Effort to Irrigate the Oklahoma Panhandle

THE DISASTROUS Mississippi River flood, the Colorado River Compact and the congressional battle to authorize a multi-purpose dam on that river, plus the Muscle Shoals controversy on the Tennessee River helped to bring the need for managing and controlling rivers to national attention in the 1920s. The 1927 Mississippi River flood made imperative the prevention of destruction on the lower Mississippi as well as its tributary streams. The "levees only" policy had failed, and a new approach was deemed necessary, an approach that recognized flood control as a national problem to be resolved by national legislation and expanded national authority.

The Flood Control Act, approved on May 15, 1928, directed the Secretary of War, through the Corps of Engineers, "to prepare and submit to Congress at the earliest possible date" flood control projects on all tributary streams of the Mississippi River that were subject to destructive floods. The Arkansas River was mentioned specifically. Congressman Everette Burgess Howard noted that losses in his state of Oklahoma totaled $20 million with floodwaters covering 762,000 acres.[1]

On July 29, 1935, the Secretary of War transmitted to the Speaker of the House of Representatives the Corps of Engineers' comprehensive study of the Arkansas River and its tributaries. Published subsequently as House Document 308 in three volumes and referred to as "The Arkansas 308 Report," it was the starting point for a discussion of the development of the river. Major dam sites were identified, estimates were offered for construction and related costs, and possible benefits were calculated. The report called for three dams on the North Canadian River, to "provide complete flood control" for this tributary and "contribute materially to flood control on the Arkansas River. The Optima Reservoir would be formed by an earthen dam 65 feet in height and 4,200 feet in length with a capacity of 77,500 acre feet." The Optima site was located approximately two and one-half miles south and one and one-half miles east of the town of Optima in Texas County in the central part of the Oklahoma Panhandle where the North Canadian was, and still is, known as the Beaver River.[2]

When Congress enacted the Flood Control Act of June 22, 1936, it authorized the construction of numerous dams and reservoirs.[3] Optima Dam was one of many called for during the New Deal to manage America's waterways and to cope, particularly in the West, with drought and dust. But when the Corps of Engineers began considering the Optima project, they discovered that the inadequate maps used and the survey made were in error as to the possible capacity of the reservoir. They believed it would be inadequate to control floods originating above the dam site. As a result, the chief of engineers, who had the authority to modify authorized projects, moved the site of the Optima Reservoir approximately twelve miles downstream from the original site to a point below the mouth of Coldwater Creek, a major tributary of the Beaver River.[4]

The cost of the reservoir was estimated at $22.7 million in the 1950s. By that time both the Corps of Engineers and the Bureau of Reclamation had made studies in connection with Optima—the corps from the standpoint of flood control and the bureau from that of irrigation. In addition, seeking to determine the best plan for control of the North Canadian River, the corps developed a four-project comprehensive plan that included the Optima, Fort Supply, and Canton reservoirs and the Oklahoma City Floodway. By 1958 the three other units had been constructed, leaving only Optima to complete the plan.[5]

However, the Optima project, after a review by the chief of engineers in 1950, was placed on inactive status because the benefit-cost ratios were estimated to be .87 to 1, or .13 below unity. Nevertheless, in its budget for the 1959 Appropriation Act, the corps set aside $25,000 to advance the project by calling for a construction design, providing the project had economic justification. Here Senator Robert S. Kerr would play a pivotal role.[6]

Elected in 1948, Kerr became deeply involved in pouring federal funds into Oklahoma water projects. In 1955 he became chairman of the Subcommittee on Flood Control and Rivers of the Senate Public Works Committee. He had secured membership on public works as well as on the finance committee when he entered the Senate. From the 1950s until his sudden death on New Year's Day 1963, he was one of the most powerful members ever to serve in that august body. His most useful power base emanated from chairing the Subcommittee on Flood Control and Rivers because it made him an ex-officio member of the

Senate Appropriations Committee (with full voting rights) and the Appropriations Conference Committee. Thus, he was in a position to further all Oklahoma projects, especially the Arkansas Navigation Project, which he co-sponsored with John McClellan, chairman of the Public Works Committee.[7]

Unfortunately, Kerr could do little for Optima because the project had to be reconfigured once the site shifted to the mouth of Coldwater Creek. From the original plan of an earth-fill dam 65 feet in height and 4,200 feet in length, it would now be about 85 feet high and 10,800 feet long. The balancing of the cost-to-benefit ratio remained the basic problem. One way to achieve balance, suggested by the district engineer, was to secure more complete studies of the project's irrigation features from the Bureau of Reclamation. To maintain stable land use, the bureau initially considered 6,000 acres as feasible for irrigation. But in the 1950s it had yet to recommend construction of the project under applicable provisions of reclamation law.[8]

Kerr and other officials suggested increased public support was needed from Panhandle residents and others who saw the Optima Dam as necessary to further flood control, to retard siltation, and to maintain more constant water storage further downstream at the Fort Supply and Canton reservoirs. Closer to the project, the Tri-State Chamber of Commerce sought to convince officials in Oklahoma City, in Tulsa, where the corps maintained its district headquarters, and in Washington, DC, of the desirability, usefulness, and vital concern of Optima to residents. Members of the chamber represented neighboring counties in

Kansas and Texas plus the three Panhandle counties and adjacent Harper County.

In its resolutions the chamber justified the project on the basis of its multiple purposes: flood control, "probable irrigation," municipal water supply, silt control, and recreation. As others outside the Panhandle observed, Optima could prevent the inundation of valuable farmland farther downstream and stabilize water storage at the two other reservoirs as part of an integrated system of flood control. If this approach were pursued, the cost-benefit ratio would be easily balanced. In giving its unqualified support to the project, the Tri-State Chamber of Commerce called for an appropriation of not less than $3 million for the preparation and commencement of construction of the Optima Dam.[9]

The chamber's resolutions were soon followed by a letter from the engineer for Texas and Cimarron counties to the concerned members of Congress from Oklahoma. He mentioned many benefits to the counties envisioned by the Tri-State Chamber of Commerce, adding, "In the future, electrical power could be developed."[10] Beginning in the 1950s local pressure for Optima began to accelerate. The classic iron triangle usually started with local groups and ended with congressional pressure on government agencies. In this case the triangle was, in effect, reversed. First, the Corps of Engineers located the site. The proposal was invigorated as Senator Kerr emerged as the dominant figure on water policy. Finally, in part because of his urging, local groups and individuals became involved.

Local interest in Optima fully emerged in the 1950s when drought and dust returned to the Oklahoma Panhandle, along with growing prosperity thanks to the development of the greatest known sweet gas reserve in the world in Texas and Beaver counties. In addition, the Panhandle was among the fastest growing areas in the Southwest. Every town had more than doubled its population since the 1940 census, and the area remained one of the nation's great wheat belts. Nevertheless, agriculture was undergoing marked changes with the appearance of feedlots and the opening of a packing plant in Guymon. Although farmers kept cover crops on their fields, the reappearance of hot winds, dust, and drought led most people in the Panhandle to support Optima more for its envisioned recreational opportunities than for any interest in flood control. Moreover, as members of the Beaver County Chamber of Commerce learned, the underground water table in their portion of the High Plains was sinking at the rate of one or two feet per year. Water depletion was now another reason to urge completion of the Optima project.[11]

In February 1950, a delegation from the Tri-State Chamber of Commerce, accompanied by Congressman George Howard Wilson, whose district included the Panhandle, testified before the Senate Appropriations Committee. Senator Kerr supported the Optima appropriation, stressing flood control. His colleague Elmer Thomas, who chaired the Appropriations Committee, believed that the Optima Dam would be given consideration. Delegation members stressed recreation and the belief that the reservoir program could "prevent a repetition of the dust bowl days," suggesting that perhaps "its greatest value [would] be its effect upon recharge of the groundwater supplies." In short, the project would provide an ideal playground and a drought-proof water supply. Thanks to the appearance of members from the Tri-State group and the support of Senator Kerr, the appropriation to get Optima off the drawing boards seemed headed for approval.[12]

Complications arose, however. The irrigation storage capacity in Optima was proposed without a plan for how the water should be used. Upon further investigation, the corps determined that no method of operating the Optima Reservoir could reduce the flood-storage requirement in downstream reservoirs on the North Canadian River. Thus, the fiscally conservative Eisenhower administration decided that construction of Optima would not begin in the near future, much to the consternation of people in the Panhandle and surrounding counties in Texas and Kansas.[13]

The project was stalled but far from over. People in the area saw it as a way of improving the quality of life, and most important, Senator Kerr still supported it. From this point on, a more standard iron triangle would operate with local groups and prominent citizens urging Kerr to secure funding and pressure the corps to get construction underway. But Kerr had to combat the opposition of the Eisenhower administration, which succeeded in having the project taken off the active list. Without the endorsement of either the corps or the Bureau of the Budget, Kerr recognized that getting consideration would be almost

impossible. However, he assured supporters of the project that
he intended "to put forth a concerted effort to secure appropriations" while hoping that local efforts would be increased and
that the project's sponsors would contact members of the Oklahoma Planning and Resources Board, urging them to get
squarely behind Optima.[14]

With dust storms, falling agricultural prices, drought, and
increasing unemployment abundantly evident by 1956, the
clamor mounted for a small appropriation to start the project.
Mike Grey, a Guymon druggist and chairman of the Democratic Party's District Central Committee, told Kerr that the governor had assured him the Planning and Resources Board would
consider the project at its next meeting. In addition, Grey con-
ferred with Colonel W. J. Hines, the district engineer in Tulsa,
who informed him that the engineering plans had been completed. All that was needed was an appropriation. Letters to Kerr
and Representative Victor Wickersham strongly reinforced interest in Optima as a way of alleviating economic conditions by
providing employment and eventually encouraging both conservation and industry. As Kerr desired, supporters also mentioned
flood control and the fact that Optima was part of the plan for
the control and development of the North Canadian River that
the Oklahoma Planning and Resources Board adopted in 1942,
the year Kerr was elected governor. Congress later reaffirmed
the plan in legislation in 1950.[15]

For his part, Kerr continually mentioned Optima in his plans
for Oklahoma projects. People and organizations in the Panhan-

dle besieged their senators and representatives in 1959 with letters and resolutions requesting the Corps of Engineers to include sufficient storage to provide for municipal and industrial water in their restudy of the project. At least eight communities endorsed this proposal, believing that the inclusion of a water supply would add greatly to the benefits of the project. The concerned members of the Oklahoma delegation in Washington agreed that the action taken by these Panhandle towns was timely and appropriate.[16]

To the charge that groundwater could supply several communities and thus obviate the need for redesigning the project, the executive director of the Oklahoma Water Resources Board informed the district engineer in Tulsa that his agency hoped groundwater could be reserved for future emergencies. However, corps studies in 1960 showed that water storage in Optima was not warranted.[17]

With the Kennedy administration and Democratic control of Congress, the bottleneck of opposition was broken. Unfortunately, Kerr did not live to see the completion of the project he had so faithfully supported; that remained for his successor, Fred Harris, and Senator Mike Monroney.

Interest in the Optima project did not abate in the 1960s, primarily because of mounting concern about depletion of the Ogallala Aquifer, the vast underground reservoir. Support for the project was fully endorsed by the district office of the Corps of Engineers in Tulsa. By 1965 some opposition was expressed by landowners whose property would be appropriated. Most people, however, were enthused about the anticipated benefits that would occur once the lake behind the dam was operative. It would back water ten miles on the Beaver River and nine miles on Coldwater Creek. The deepest point would be more than one hundred feet. People in the tri-state region could look forward to water skiing, sail and speed boat racing, and warm-water fishing. Plans included picnic areas, possible summer camps, and a mecca for ducks and geese. All of these recreational benefits were in addition to the more obvious gain from flood control. Economic assets after completion would help ensure an ever-growing tourist industry and the businesses catering to it. All of these points and numerous others were listed in a brochure widely distributed by the Guymon Chamber of Commerce.[18]

The ten thousand acres needed for the project were owned by thirty-two people and the state. Families whose property would be consumed by the project bitterly protested: circulating petitions, writing letters, and arguing with friends, neighbors, and anyone who would listen. One desperate individual wrote Senator Harris that "families are being divided, people are removing their deposits from banks." Schools, churches, and civic clubs were being disrupted. This embittered individual concluded, "We are going, or have gone, Communist."[19]

Other opponents were more rational in their opposition. One critic claimed the dam would only be full once every ten years and no farmer could irrigate from such an uncertain supply. Moreover, cities and towns could "drill wells much cheaper and have clean water." And the dam would take more land out of production than it would save from floods. The chief thrust of the project's supporters was recreation; this critic thought "that $23,000,000 is a big price to pay for just a place to play."[20]

A spate of letters both positive and negative poured in to members of the Oklahoma delegation and the governor as it became evident that Congress might now authorize funding for Optima. This outpouring was prompted in part by a luncheon speaker at the Guymon Kiwanis Club who asked for a letter-writing campaign voicing opinions, either pro or con, on the project. In a form letter to constituents who had expressed opposition, Fred Harris wrote that after studying the purposes and feasibility of the project, he deemed it worthy of support. He did so because of the benefits that would accrue from flood protection, water and soil conservation, a municipal water supply, and recreation throughout the entire North Canadian Valley. Harris hoped to see the conclusion of a project that his distinguished predecessor was unable to bring to fruition.[21]

Harris's Senate colleague, Mike Monroney, received similar letters. Interest was mounting as pre-construction planning continued with funds appropriated during the Kennedy administration. The district engineer in Tulsa anticipated planning to be sufficiently advanced by the end of fiscal year 1965 to permit advertising for initial construction once Congress appropriated funds. Toward this end Harris endorsed the Optima project before both the House and Senate Appropriations Subcommittees on Public Works. The total estimated federal cost would be $23.1 million. Already $585,000 had been used for preconstruction planning. Harris respectfully requested that $1.2 million be included in fiscal year 1966 appropriations to initiate construction. All concerned were optimistic that funds would be forthcoming and that construction would get underway. This was related to the determination of Senator John McClellan, chair of the Public Works Committee, to keep the Arkansas River Navigation Project on schedule for completion in 1970. It was of vital interest to the people of Arkansas and Oklahoma; Optima, in effect, would piggyback on this massive project.[22]

While Harris appeared before congressional committees, Mike Monroney toured the Panhandle. He told constituents that the benefit-cost ratio had improved since communities in the vicinity of the reservoir had informed the Corps of Engineers that they endorsed the project primarily to secure an assured municipal water supply. It now stood at $1.21 for each dollar invested by the federal government. However, a spokesman for the corps explained to Monroney that there was no money in the president's budget to launch the project. Therefore, like Harris, Monroney promised residents that he would endeavor to secure funds to initiate construction. He was convinced that development of Optima represented progress toward the conservation and utilization of precious water sources.[23]

Once the project was restudied in 1962 and its economic feasibility affirmed, planning was resumed with funds appropriated in fiscal year 1963. Fiscal year 1965 funds completed the preconstruction planning. In 1966 construction got underway when Congress, defying the president's budget, appropriated funds for that specific purpose. Neither Harris nor Monroney were serving in the Senate when the Corps of Engineers completed the project in 1978. The cost, far exceeding all previous estimates, was $46,111,000. The dam is a rolled-earth fill structure 15,200 feet long and rises 120 feet above the streambed. The emergency spillway is 1,500 feet wide and has a capacity of 359,000 cubic feet per second (cfs) at maximum pool elevations. However, up to the present day, the conservation pool has yet to fill. The lake was authorized for flood control, water supply, recreation, and fish and wildlife purposes. Yet the Oklahoma Water Resources Board, in updating its Comprehensive Water Plan in 1995, stated, "There is no dependable water supply yield in Optima at this time."[24]

Seemingly, the Optima project, first authorized in the Flood Control Act of 1936, was a disastrous $46 million mistake. It did not adequately fulfill any of its purposes. The High Plains region, including the Oklahoma Panhandle, is subject to prolonged periods of insufficient water interspersed with infrequent periods of far too much. To help control this situation, the Corps of Engineers constructed two reservoirs at Canton and Fort Supply on the North Canadian River. A third was deemed necessary in the Panhandle, a region that suffered severely during the years of depression, drought, and dust. This vision remained vivid to those in and out of government who clamored for the construction of Optima. It promised a new day for residents of the region, and Oklahoma political musclemen exerted their collective efforts to make the dream a reality. Led by Senator Kerr, they already had made Oklahoma the home of numerous state and federal water projects. Unfortunately, the semi-arid Panhandle was not that lucky. Its generally flat lands, low runoff, and high evaporation made it poorly suited to reservoir construction. Water evaporation, enhanced by strong winds, generally far exceeded the average yearly rainfall. Though lacking in surface water, the region's residents were beginning by the 1970s to tap into the tremendous but finite groundwater resources of the Ogallala Aquifer, which, among other things, supports irrigation and feed-lot operations. Texas County, where Optima is located, is the largest water user among Oklahoma's seventy-seven counties.

In a visit to Optima Lake in August 1998, I found the welcome center locked. No ranger was in sight. A brochure available in a box outside the center stated, "The lake has not reached normal levels and may not be suitable for all types of boating." The brochure contained photos of water-skiers, children on a sunny beach, and a family enjoying a sunset at water's edge with a motorboat nearby. The reality I observed was a desolate area with nary a soul in sight and a lake with tree stumps and other debris clearly evident. The lake area provides opportunities for hunters, though fishermen could have problems. In short, while the project might serve several useful purposes, the vast benefits envisioned for the project by people in the Panhandle and neighboring areas in Texas and Kansas were never realized and remain at best a $46 million pipe dream.

From Petroleum to Pigs

The Oklahoma Panhandle in the Last Half of the Twentieth Century

DESPITE ADVERSE weather conditions in the 1950s and 1970s, the Oklahoma Panhandle in the years following World War II experienced enhanced prosperity. And beginning in the 1950s, themes evident in the previous decade and even earlier came to the forefront and markedly diversified the economic base of Panhandle prosperity. Still an outback with regard to the rest of Oklahoma, its degree of exceptionalism with regard to the Southern Great Plains was considerably reduced as both the Hugoton Gas Field and the Ogallala Aquifer underlay neighboring states as well. Both gas and water brought about similar developments in southwestern Kansas, in parts of the Texas Panhandle, and to a much lesser degree in southeastern Colorado and northeastern New Mexico. But the changes were more pronounced in the area comprising the three counties of the Oklahoma Panhandle. As it had at the outset of statehood, the population of the Panhandle remained sparse. Texas County continued as the county most favored by new developments—oil and gas production, irrigation, feedlots, a packing plant, and in the last decade of the twentieth century, pig farms. While these new developments are interrelated, each will need separate explication.

Initially, a large part of the natural gas produced in Oklahoma was wasted. Because it was produced in connection with oil and could not easily be stored, it was allowed to escape into the air. But by the 1950s when the Hugoton Field, the largest known gas-producing area in the world, was developed, that was no longer the case. Guymon soon was known as the "Sweet Gas Capital of the World." In 1958 Texas County's 1,373 gas wells produced approximately 70 billion cubic feet of gas per month. Conservation engineers testified to reserves of trillions of feet. Soon the county and to a much lesser extent the neighboring counties were dotted with gas-field satellite companies and gas-well servicing companies. In Beaver County, the Crown Ranch sat on top of another large natural gas field. There were five producing wells on the ranch. These discoveries changed the Panhandle area from a predominately agricultural region to one of industrial development.[1]

Oil was discovered in the Eva area of Texas County, northwest of Guymon, in 1953. Soon thereafter several oil companies operated some fifty wells in the field. Southeast of Guymon, in the same year, both oil and gas were discovered in the vast Camrick Field at a depth of about 6,700 feet. In Cimarron County, there were about 250 producing wells yielding gas from a depth of about 4,500 feet. Numerous oil strikes were prevalent with that development. In Beaver County, oil was first discovered in 1952. Since that time, practically all the major oil companies have been active with production and exploration throughout the county. In the Mocane area in the 1950s, there were some sixty wells pumping, with numerous drilling rigs running. Thus, in a radius of one hundred miles around Guymon were represented more than sixty oil and gas concerns. The effects of that development on the Panhandle economy, involving an estimated

$250 million capital expenditure, were most directly felt in Guy-mon, the geological hub of this tremendous development. Suc-cessful results in Oklahoma exploration made 1953 a banner year. Fieldwork was the heaviest in the state's history. Each year of the decade brought discoveries of more gas and oil wells, as would be the case on into the 1980s and 1990s, when production began slowly to decline. Thanks to those discoveries, landowners reaped an unexpected harvest in lease bonuses.[2]

Nevertheless, tensions quickly arose when four Texas County landowners filed a suit against the Phillips Petroleum Company seeking a permanent injunction enjoining Phillips from cutting off their supply of gas for pumping irrigation wells. The four wells involved were not under contract for gas to Phillips, but Phillips threatened to cut off their supply on the grounds that the gas was dedicated for pipeline purposes and could not be used indefinitely to service irrigation pumps even though the large landowners were willing to pay the prevailing price for gas. The application for an injunction was based on an Oklahoma law stating that a pipeline company had to provide gas to landowners whose acres company pipelines crossed. Phillips objected because it did not want its gas sales subject to public regulation. Since Phillips controlled 285,000 acres of the Hugo-ton Gas Field in 1960, the matter was of some concern. It sold its gas to pipeline companies and most likely resolved the fears of irrigators because the issue never cropped up again. But irri-gators were still concerned about the activities of oil and gas pro-ducers in the Panhandle.[3]

In two cases decided by the Oklahoma Supreme Court, Texas County irrigators tried to curb the activities of oil companies, claiming they were polluting fresh groundwater for the purpose of secondary (in a 1977 case) and secondary and tertiary (in a 1984 case) water-flood operations to recover oil. In both cases, which involved the Texas County Irrigation and Water Resources Association, the court found with some dissent that when fresh groundwater was withdrawn, neither waste by pollution nor waste by depletion would occur. While irrigators soon were able to use natural gas to pump their wells, their efforts to curb oil and gas producers from using fresh groundwater to flush their wells for further oil recovery failed.[4]

Meanwhile, oil and gas corporations continued to invest in the Panhandle, constructing plants and pipelines delivering billions of cubic feet of natural gas to companies and consumers throughout mid-America. Beaver County was the site of many of those activities as numerous corporations appeared to develop the Mocane-Laverne Field, which soon rivaled the Hugoton Field as a major energy source. In the Keyes area of Cimarron County, a huge reserve of helium-bearing gas attracted the attention of the federal government. It was one of the richest helium-containing gas deposits in the world. Helium played a prominent role in operating atomic reactors, rockets, and missiles. To meet increased demand prompted by Cold War defense needs of the armed services as well as the weather bureau, the Bureau of Mines sought to construct a plant to produce helium. In 1958 the Department of the Interior signed a long-term contract with the Colorado Interstate Gas Company, giving the

Bureau of Mines exclusive rights to extract helium from natural gas produced by the company in the Keyes Field. An extraction plant was in operation by the end of the following year. With a capacity of 290 million cubic feet of helium per year, it was the largest extraction plan operated by the Bureau of Mines. By 1964 the Keyes plant produced more than 6 percent of the national yield of helium.[5]

The giant gas fields (Camrick, Mocane-Laverne, and Hugoton), plus processing plants, the giant Postle Oil Field in Texas County, the helium plant near Keyes, and other areas of oil and gas production were centrally located in Beaver and Texas counties. The Oklahoma Panhandle from Beaver through eastern Cimarron County presented a vast surface-portrait of wells, processing plants, and gas pipes. Pipelines from the Hugoton Field took natural gas to consumers in Nebraska, Iowa, Minnesota, and South Dakota. Other lines pumped gas to the Northeast. Only a small amount was consumed close at hand. The Postle Oil Field, largely undeveloped until the 1970s, contained 313 wells producing almost 4 million barrels by 1977. Its cumulative production was over 84 million barrels, and its reserves were estimated at almost 36 million barrels. In 1975 it was ranked among the top 100 producing pools in the nation. Indeed, on into the 1980s new oil and gas wells were being brought into production throughout the Panhandle. In Beaver County Texaco and the Warren Petroleum Corporation constructed deep underground caverns for storage of barrels of liquefied petroleum gas.[6]

By any standard, production of oil and gas in the Panhandle

was impressive. From 1979 to 1993 in Beaver County, total oil production amounted to 39,744,667 barrels; for natural gas the figure was 1,316,791,103 cubic feet. For Texas County the figures were 58,643,167 barrels and 1,753,018,669 cubic feet. For Cimarron County they totaled 7,411,981 barrels and 205,060,403 cubic feet. In 1997 there were 2,330 producing leases in Beaver County, 2,333 in Texas County, and 186 in Cimarron County. Income from gas and oil leases enabled many Panhandle farmers to withstand declining crop prices and crop failures. As the century came to an end, oil and gas production in the Oklahoma Panhandle, although declining, was far from depleted. Production began to decrease moderately as fields matured and supply emphasis shifted from domestic to foreign sources, but pump jacks continued to share the landscape with grain elevators and windmills.[7]

Those pump jacks prompted marked changes in land use with regard to cattle and crops in the postwar years. Agriculture, despite prodigious energy development, remained the basic industry and was central to the way of life in the Oklahoma Panhandle. Most people continued to derive their livelihood from agriculture. Oil and gas production prompted irrigation and the tapping of the Ogallala Aquifer. Irrigation allowed the production of row crops—corn and grain sorghums—to compete with wheat as the leading crop. Row crops provided feed for livestock, which led to the creation of feedlots and the construction of a packing plant in the Panhandle. And by the end of the century, a totally new development—pig farms—made its appearance. Guymon remained the center for these new developments, as it had been in the production of natural gas and petroleum, and the county maintained its position as the heart of the Panhandle. So it was at statehood, thanks to the railroad, and so it remained at the end of the century.

Ranchers and farmers continued to share the land in almost equal proportions. Large farms and large ranches experiencing limited rainfall and long hot summers kept their owners almost continuously worried about drought. But the situation had changed markedly from the Dust Bowl days. Few were the acres without cover crops, and almost every land user employed conservation techniques and practices such as leaving wheat stubble on the field, strip farming, terracing, and retiring tilled land to grass to protect the soil from erosion.

Farmers and ranchers were doing their best to cooperate with nature. Although the area experienced severe drought in the 1950s, arguably more severe than that of the 1930s, the impact was minimal thanks to improved farming methods to control wind erosion, oil and gas leases, and the beginning of extensive irrigation. Comparatively mild dust storms emanated chiefly from West Texas and Colorado. They were limited to a few days, and the drought, which attracted national attention, was not a major factor. In no noticeable way did it seriously impede the changes underway in the 1950s. However, a severe blizzard caused serious damage in March 1957, wreaking havoc on life and property, downing power lines, blocking roads, stalling trains, killing cattle, and blowing out wheat.[8]

Large farms remained the rule rather than the exception in the postwar years. The average farm encompassed more than a square mile of territory; neighbors were few and far between. The Panhandle was a sparsely populated land slowly losing people. Population density in the 1970s was less than ten people per square mile. In 1990, for the first time, Texas County had a population slightly higher than at statehood in 1907. Beaver and Cimarron counties had not yet reached that point. The western edge of the Panhandle, dotted with sagebrush and tumbleweeds, remained grazing country. Expansion of cropland into rangeland was impractical, since rough terrain or sandy soil precluded adequate crop returns.[9] Therefore, grazing displaced farming in spots only where broken and rough lands existed. This happened frequently, though, as there were almost 2 million acres of cropland and 1.75 million acres of rangeland.

By 1977 over 270,000 acres of farmland were irrigated, more than the rest of Oklahoma combined, though dryland farming still predominated. Usually, only part of a farm was irrigated. Gravity irrigation was important in Cimarron and Texas counties; sprinkler irrigation was more evident in Beaver County. Deep well drilling needed natural gas for pumping, and nearly all farms had natural gas piped from a well on the farm. Given the amount of irrigation, concern was expressed about lowering the water table. Some irrigators, led by H. C. "Ladd" Hitch, the owner of a large ranch near Guymon and son of Henry C. Hitch, called for a cloud-seeding project but found little support for the idea. Panhandle ranchers and farmers also expressed interest in devising a method of utilizing Oklahoma's surplus water, but a water-transfer plan was never developed despite an abundance of water in the eastern, "green" part of the state.[10]

The expanding use of water markedly changed Panhandle agriculture beginning in the 1950s. The adoption of irrigation technology supported a steady upward trend in irrigated acres until the 1980s, when energy costs for lifting water from increasing depths rose in an agricultural market of stable or declining commodity prices. Moreover, as the amount of pumping increased, the depth to the water also increased. By 1980 there were more than 2,000 wells scattered throughout the Oklahoma Panhandle yielding from 500 to 1,000 gallons per minute. Declines in water level meant a decrease in the rate at which water pumps delivered water, an increase in pumping costs, and possible water-quality problems from saline encroachment. Utilizing groundwater required a permit from the Oklahoma Water Resources Board. By 1975 the board had granted 1,577 groundwater permits. At that time the Ogallala Aquifer contained about 46 million acre-feet of available water. It was used to irrigate more than 400,000 acres of agricultural land and to meet other needs in the region. In 1996 it had an estimated storage of 112 million acre-feet.[11]

The average cost of drilling a 400- to 500-foot well, leveling land, installing pumps, and preparing ditches could run anywhere from $9,000 to $16,000 per establishment. In the 1950s, irrigated acreage in the Panhandle expanded about 8 percent a year. And the outlook was so good that one operator in 1959 believed the costs would be amortized within ten years. By the 1970s, as irrigation continued to increase, the availability and price of fuel to power pumps became a matter of concern. Without natural gas, the irrigation boom that began in the 1950s probably would never have taken place. After the Arab oil embargo and a 1975 decision of the Federal Power Commission that awarded natural gas for agricultural use a low priority, Panhandle irrigators worked hard to raise their priority level. As mentioned previously, they were forced to fight large corporations that piped natural gas from the Panhandle to other areas. These companies attempted to deny irrigators the right to the gas they had been utilizing, which, in many instances, was produced from under the irrigators' own land.[12]

Fears about declining water levels were abated early in 1971 when an Oklahoma Agricultural Experiment Station study assured Panhandle residents utilizing the Central Ogallala Formation that they need not curtail irrigation. Economists predicted that Central Ogallala irrigation would increase from 1.6 million acres in 1971 to a peak of 3.4 million acres by the end of the century, after which an overall decline would begin. This meant that the quantity of water withdrawn from the aquifer would increase from 2.8 million acre-feet to a peak of about 6 million acre-feet in the 1990s. Thereafter, water use would decrease rapidly.

But in the 1970s no wells had gone dry; no drilling had tapped the aquifer's lower limits; and there was no sense of crisis. Water remained the secret to prosperity in the Panhandle.

New methods and new crops appeared. Center-pivot irrigation saved both labor and water. Dirt ditches with water running from siphon tubes gave way to circle systems. Sprinklers helped make alfalfa a practical crop to irrigate. As hay, it became a staple of feedlot operations along with grain sorghums and corn silage. With four or five harvests a season, alfalfa was an attractive crop for irrigation farmers. Although barley challenged wheat, it never replaced wheat as the basic market crop, even though some farmers used everything they produced as cattle feed. And some irrigators looked at soybeans as a rotation crop with corn, grain sorghum, and wheat. Others considered utilizing underground pipe and a system to catch tail water from wells. In one instance, this practice pumped 700 to 800 gallons a minute at a lower cost than operating another well.[13]

By the 1980s, over 25 percent of wheat, 50 percent of grain sorghums, and almost all corn and alfalfa produced in the Panhandle were irrigated. By 1988 2,600 wells were pumping water, mostly from the aquifer. An earlier press release from the Oklahoma Water Resources Board indicated "Demand For Fresh Water Soaring in Panhandle." Texas County set records among all counties for the most water used, the most water used for irrigation, and the most acres irrigated. Cimarron County was fifth among all counties in the three categories. Beaver County lagged far behind in its water use and high-capacity well development. While the board was concerned about declining water levels, it did little more than document the declension in its water plans.[14]

As discussed previously, one proposal that boded great

promise turned out to be a deep and expensive disappointment to farmers and ranchers eager for an abundance of cheap water. A dam and reservoir near the town of Optima on the Beaver River was authorized in 1936, funds were appropriated in 1962, and construction began in 1966. The Optima project was completed by the Corps of Engineers in 1978 at a cost of over $46 million, but it was soon evident the project did not fulfill its promise. The conservation pool has yet to fill. Since its construction there has been no dependable water-supply yield in Optima. Reasons advanced for its construction have either been realized minimally or not at all. Underground water, ever being diminished, remains the primary source of water in the Panhandle.[15]

Until the 1970s, when center-pivot and wheel-line irrigation came into use, the three general ways of irrigating soils were by flooding, by furrows, or by sprinklers. Despite this expansion in irrigation, grazing competed with wheat as the chief use of land. In the 1960s, there were sixteen ranches utilizing over twenty-five sections, or 15,000 acres each. The largest of the ranches covered 137 sections in Beaver County and spilled over into an adjoining eastern county. In Texas County, there were sixty livestock ranches averaging about 3,500 acres in size. Numerous smaller ranches, occupying five to twenty-five sections, were interspersed with the larger ranches in the areas of rolling topography bordering the Beaver and Cimarron rivers and their major tributaries. Cimarron County had the highest percentage of its land in pasture, about 650,000 acres; Texas County, the smallest. In northwestern Cimarron County much of the land was not suitable for cultivation and was never claimed, or if claimed, it was abandoned and had reverted to the state. Such land, often deemed suitable for grazing, was rented to ranchers for thirty to sixty cents per acre per year. Since a rancher could rent the land in many instances for less than what the taxes would be, several ranchers rented considerably more land than they owned. Although carrying capacity varied, it generally allowed more than fifteen and sometimes as much as fifty acres per cow. Rarely was any animal more than a mile from water, making windmills and watering troughs ever-present features of the landscape. A newer development in the 1950s was dairying. In Beaver County, for example, there were ninety Grade A dairies. Dairy farmers made determined efforts to improve their pastures by planting more luxuriant and enriching seeds in addition to conserving native grasses for proper pasturing methods.[16]

Most ranchers followed a conservation program to control the number of livestock on the range so that at least half the yearly growth of plants was left ungrazed. Most ranchers at one time or another worked with agents of their Soil Conservation District. Deferred grazing, or leaving some pasture idle in the summer, helped seriously depleted range to recover more rapidly. Brush and weeds that impaired forage production were controlled through chemicals or mowing. Ranchers understood that the improvement of native vegetation assured the production of range forage and the conservation of plants, soil, and water. Large upland areas, notable in Texas and Cimarron counties, had no adequate drainage. Although playas were numerous, they only retained water during and after rainy seasons unless nourished by irrigation runoff. After a thunderstorm, nearly 600 water-filled playas could spangle the three counties, but only a handful survived for significant periods. An exceptional playa was Wildhorse Lake in Texas County. Its owners modified it to store irrigation water all year round. Originally covering 120 acres, the playa was deepened by a 30-acre hole that reduced the water surface to 34 acres, to collect water from a 22,000-acre watershed.[17]

While playas benefited both farmers and ranchers, well water, allowing for the planting of feed crops, brought about fundamental changes in the way cattle were processed. Feedlots were beginning to appear in the Oklahoma Panhandle in the 1950s. An increase in feedlot capacity encouraged ranchers to graze more with cattle, while irrigated corn and grain sorghums allowed them to expand their endeavors. By the 1970s feedlots were a major enterprise in the Oklahoma Panhandle as stockmen utilized feed grown in the area to fatten their cattle.[18] And by the 1980s, beef markets for cattle raised on the Southern High Plains were no longer centralized in Kansas City and Denver. Once corn could be grown in the area, the markets moved to be concentrated in the Oklahoma and Texas panhandles and southwestern Kansas. Operators who were both farmers and ranchers could then bring greater diversity to their operations. While government subsidies encouraged farmers to concentrate on grain farming, market pressures determined land use for ranchers more so than government subsidies. Farmers could possibly secure greater yields through the application of science, technology, and improved irrigation, but ranchers required more land to stock their pastures with more cattle to meet the needs of a supply-and-demand market and to maintain an adequate acreage-per-animal unit to prevent overgrazing.

Cattle development was further facilitated when Swift and Company constructed a packing plant in Guymon. The company was lured to the community by a new air-conditioned livestock auction facility and a huge new feedlot adjacent to the facility. Moreover, through a survey taken by county agents within a 100-mile radius, it was determined there were 1,533,050 acres of irrigated farmland growing enough feed to fatten 898,600 head of cattle. The packing plant opened for business on September 5, 1967, and was soon slaughtering 2,500 head of cattle a week and shipping to outlets throughout the nation. In April of the following year, the plant processed 3,911 head a week, and by 1973, it had an annual capacity of over 200,000 head. That operation gave substantial impetus to feedlot development and helped to make the area one of the largest beef-producing centers in the nation. The plant operated at close to capacity, making it one of the early developments in the meat-packing industry's move to the new beef belt in the Southwest. And it provided a terminal market in the middle of the Panhandle.[19]

Many Panhandle stockmen then shifted from producing feeder cattle, which were placed in a feedlot for fattening, to finished cattle, which were sent to a feedlot prior to being slaughtered. A new feedlot could handle between 10,000 and 16,000 head of cattle and was a valuable source of fertilizer for the stockmen. Feedlots were usually commercial enterprises, but the Hitch family provided its own. On any given day its three feed-lots could hold up to 160,000 cattle purchased from smaller pro-ducers. The family's 10,000-acre farming operation provided grain sorghum feed for the cattle, which were either sold to Swift and Company and other nearby packinghouses or processed by Booker Custom Packing, a family-owned meat-packing com-pany. The market for Panhandle beef was largely to the south and east of Oklahoma, including the Gulf Coast.[20]

The commercial lots did not own the cattle, but they did pro-vide space, feed, and medical care for the animals in return for a fee. Panhandle feedlots drew cattle primarily from Oklahoma and Texas. The cattle remained in the lots anywhere from 120 to 150 days. Feeders, mixing grain and silage, hoped that an animal would gain at least 300 pounds to attract buyers from packing companies, who purchased them either by grade and yield or on the hoof. Trucks carried cattle from the ranch to the lot and from there to the slaughterhouse. Even with a packing plant in Guy-mon, Panhandle feedlots sold cattle in 1966 to sixteen different packing companies. The Oklahoma Panhandle thus supported a multiple-stage industry that took feeder calves and transformed them into grain-finished beef. Hitch Enterprises in Texas County and Roy T. Nall in Cimarron County in the 1970s man-aged two of the Panhandle's major cattle-feeding operations.[21]

So noticeable were those developments that by the 1970s hundreds of visitors from as far away as Korea, Japan, and Argentina, from nearby Nebraska and Kansas, and from all over Oklahoma came to see for themselves. Few, if any, of the tourists ventured into Cimarron County to view a new development that would attract even more attention by the end of century. The MPF hog-feeding lot differed minimally from other feedlots. The feeding facility consisted of a 1,500-foot, open-to-the-south shed from which thirty pens extended. Each pen held 100 hogs ranging from 40-pound pigs to 220-pound hogs ready to go to market, either to a killing plant in Amarillo or to a gathering point at Woodward, Oklahoma, and then on to Wichita or Kansas City.[22]

In 1972 most of the pigs came from Arkansas. The operators could take a local pig up to 220 pounds in 90 to 110 days; those from Arkansas took 10 to 20 days longer to reach the same weight. But hog feeding was still a precarious operation, and few, if any, Panhandle stockmen sought to emulate the MPF operation. However, within two decades, that situation had markedly changed. By the 1990s, pork palaces abounded in the Oklahoma Panhandle.[23]

In 1992 the Census of Agriculture indicated that only 31,274 hogs were marketed in Texas County. Four years later, John Fraser Hart and Chris Mayda wrote, "the Panhandle was plastered with proliferating pork palaces with their unpainted metal roofs shimmering in the sun." Texas County again took the lead, producing 2 million hogs and becoming the focal point of an area that produced 4 percent of the national total, about 4 million hogs.

Each hog farm, a cluster of two to ten long, narrow, level

structures of gleaming white sheet metal, was constructed in rigid rows on dry ground in the niches between croplands on which effluent was pumped. Beside each building, cylindrical metal bins with cone-shaped bottoms carried feed through spidery tubes to all the hogs in the structure at the touch of a button. Manure was flushed into a "lagoon," where the solids settled and the liquid evaporated, creating an objectionable odor.

The entire operation was tightly organized into different clusters or units. Brood sows were in a unit for breeding, gestation, and farrowing. The pigs were weaned at fourteen days, weighing around twelve pounds, and taken to a nursery unit until they weighed about fifty pounds. Then they were hauled off to a finishing unit until they achieved a weight of 275 pounds. At the age of six and a half months they were ready for the gigantic processing plant constructed by Seaboard Farms near Guymon.

The plant could process 1,000 hogs an hour and 2 million hogs a year. It opened in December 1995; within two years it operated on two daily shifts. Seaboard was the linchpin of the vast new hog-production system. It developed its own hog farms and purchased hogs from other producers who met its standards. The company provided hogs, feed, medication, and expertise to producers who could provide land, buildings, and labor. Paul Hitch contracted with Seaboard to deliver 300,000 hogs a year, and a Spanish company developed an operation capable of producing 500,000 hogs a year. The availability of the processing plant plus the relaxation of international trade barriers attracted other hog producers to the area. Nippon Meat Packing, the fourth largest meat packing company in the world, acquired seven sections of land near Perryton, Texas. It planned to produce 500,000 hogs a year that would be processed by Seaboard and then transported by rail and ship across the Pacific to markets throughout Japan, still counter fresh after fifty days.

Seaboard came to the Panhandle for the same reasons that feedlots and packing plants arrived earlier. Ogallala water and natural gas, though declining in volume, were inexpensive. Irrigators continued to produce good crops of corn and sorghums, which provided the main feed for hog farms. While the lagoons provided a target for critics, they evaporated rapidly in the dry climate with steady winds and ample sunshine. The sparse population of the three counties also meant that there were fewer people to complain about the smell. Most Panhandle residents had been preconditioned to livestock odors from the concentration of beef-cattle feedlots, although the odor of hog manure is considered more noxious because hogs, like humans, consume concentrated food, whereas cattle ingest large quantities of roughage.

In brief, the hog industry, heavily concentrated in the Corn Belt, has rapidly moved away from its traditional structure based on small farms and local terminal markets to a vertically integrated industry. Seaboard Farms, a diversified international food-production, food-processing, and transportation entity, and its huge Guymon operation is a major player in transforming the industry.[24] Its presence helped increase pork production in Oklahoma almost 900 percent in the 1990s. Moreover, as already suggested, the Panhandle was well positioned to ship pork products to growing markets in the West Coast and Asia. And its abundant corn crop, the major ingredient in hog feed, added to the attractiveness of the area. Of the top fifteen hog producers in the nation, seven had operations in Oklahoma.

While the Panhandle was attractive to pork producers, Oklahoma was concerned about the environmental impact of the integrated industry. In June 1998, a law was enacted stipulating a new licensing process giving landowners within a mile of a hog farm a substantial voice in the granting of permits. The legislation also set clear requirements for waste disposal and mandated professional certification that waste disposal was not affecting the quality of groundwater. It imposed a fee amounting to thirty-two cents a hog to cover the costs of implementing the law. It also decreed that all new operations had to be located at least three miles from city limits and 300 feet from any well. At the time, the legislation was the most restrictive and therefore the most environmentally concerned measure affecting pork producers in the United States.[25]

The sparse population created labor housing problems in the Panhandle, especially in and around Guymon. Packinghouse workers and their families, housed mainly in mobile homes (the contemporary equivalent of the company town), helped to diminish the Caucasian complexion of Panhandle residents. Demographically, the Panhandle had always been a land of native-born whites, who made up about 99 percent of its population. In 1950 only 258 foreign-born whites and 46 members of other races lived in the area. Only 5 African Americans and 6

American Indians resided in the three counties. By 1995 two counties had a population smaller than at statehood in 1907: Beaver County went from 13,364 to 5,900, and Cimarron County from 5,927 to 3,000. Only Texas County showed an increase and a slight one at that: 16,448 to 16,800. But the ethnic diversity had markedly shifted since 1950. In 1995 the estimated census indicated that 72 African Americans, 280 American Indians, 44 Asians, and 1,408 Hispanics resided in the Panhandle. Those figures will undoubtedly increase if hog farming continues to expand and pig processing increases to even higher levels. Finally, per capita income for the three counties continues at the top levels for the state, always among the top five counties.[26]

As the twentieth century came to an end, concern about the future of the Panhandle gained intensity as the Oklahoma portion of the Ogallala Aquifer continued to recede. Thus far, no wells have gone dry, and no drilling has tapped its lower levels. In the 1970s, it was assumed the end of water from the aquifer would be evident in the 1990s. Now it is assumed it will be reached in another two to three decades. Though no new major oil or gas fields have been developed, pumper wells abound, and the depletion of the fields is not yet evident. While American consumers are not as enamored with beef as they were in the past, ranching and stockyards are still flourishing, though the Swift and Company plant is no longer operative. Pig farming is now prospering and could continue to do so in the foreseeable future. No matter what changes occur, the Oklahoma Panhandle, encompassing 8.5 percent of the state's land area and containing about 2 percent of its population, will continue to be an important agricultural area. While irrigation continues on a large scale, dryland farming still continues on an equally large scale, and wheat remains, as it has since statehood, a dominant crop. While changes will occur, owing to a depleting resource base and both national and international market factors, the land will endure, and a small rural population aided by constantly improving technology, informed scientific knowledge, and corporate and/or government guidance should be able to compete successfully and the three counties of the Oklahoma Panhandle to maintain their status among the most prosperous in the state.

Epilogue

As THE twenty-first century unfolds, the Oklahoma Panhandle remains the most prosperous part of the state, with wheat, meat, and energy the most important factors in its economy. Texas County, for example, continues as the leading gas-producing county in the nation. At the same time its agricultural industries—wheat, grain sorghums, corn, and cattle—rank among the top in the state, competing with Beaver and Cimarron counties. In 2001 Brian Mitchell's 32,000-acre family farm in the Panhandle, which produces corn, wheat, and grain sorghum, received more federal subsidies than any other agricultural operation in Oklahoma. Hitch Enterprises of Guymon received more than $900,000 in federal subsidies from grain crops on 6,000 to 7,000 acres in fiscal 2000. In addition to its farming operations, Hitch Enterprises also includes a large cattle feeding and hog production business, fattening just under 300,000 head of cattle and hogs annually for slaughter.[1]

While the Panhandle, despite the drought pervading most of the Great Plains, maintains its traditional prosperous patterns, massive and fundamental changes launched in the 1990s are significantly altering life while expanding its economic base. Responsible for this change is a 1991 law enacted by the Oklahoma legislature, which allowed corporate farming in the state. Prior to 1991 family farmers were able to incorporate their operations, but the new law permitted huge agribusiness operations to function in the state. Two years later Seaboard Farms, a diversified international agribusiness and transportation company headquartered in Shawnee Mission, Kansas, entered the Panhandle, where as previously noted, it is engaged in pork production, processing, and cargo shipping. Internationally, the corporation is involved with commodity merchandising, flour and feed milling, sugar production, and electric power generation.

Today, Seaboard operates two huge sow farms. Its Dorman Sow Farms, for example, houses about 25,000 sows capable of producing around twenty pigs each year for processing at their huge plant in Guymon. Its Wakefield Farm, also in Beaver County, operates with about 27,000 sows. Seaboard, the largest producer of swine in the state, does not contract with individual farmers for hogs; however, it does process hogs of other pig operators in the Panhandle, such as Smithfield Foods, the nation's largest pork producer. In 2002 Smithfield Foods paid Texhoma-based hog producer Vail, Inc., a subsidiary of a privately owned livestock producer in Spain, over $60 million in cash for its 20,000 sow and hog farms. It is a farm-to-finish operation in which piglets are raised to market weight and then sold to Seaboard Farms. About 350,000 hogs go annually to the Guymon packing plant for processing.[2]

In the short time it has been in the Panhandle, Seaboard has not proven itself to be environmentally friendly, though it is currently making efforts to do so. Like other large operators, it faces the problem of stanching the stench of huge hog farms. While state law requires large hog companies to pay 80 cents per large animal to the state, which uses the money to check and improve water quality, it initially imposed no requirement for installing odor abatement equipment. In December 2001 Seaboard agreed to adopt some $3 million worth of odor abatement and water quality measures. In addition, in its arrangement with the Attorney General, Seaboard promised to install a number of additional methods to control odor pollution, including a scrubber-burner system for its manure filled lagoons.[3]

Lagoons and the disposal of hog waste changes land use in areas close to large pig farms. In February 2000, Seaboard, for example, paid state fines of $22,500 for three spills at Dorman Sow Farms. Operations at its hog farms dilute the waste with millions of gallons of water collected in lagoons before being sprayed on the ground. The vital concern is whether the effluent from massive Panhandle pig farms will be absorbed and adequately used by the land or whether it will cause pollution of surface and groundwaters. If the water that seeps back into the soil is polluted, it could contaminate the rest of the groundwater. Hog farms typically use about one-third of their water for drinking by the animals; the other two-thirds is used to wash away pig manure into lagoons and eventually spread onto the land.[4]

Controversy arose when corporate hog producers pumped water from the Ogallala Aquifer, used it for swine production, and then piped the effluent into a customer's irrigation system. Then the wastewater was applied to corn and wheat fields. Farmers who use waste water in this way will be drawing less fresh water from the aquifer and eliminating the need and expense, for example, of irrigating by a center-pivot system.[5]

Using waste water to curb the use of groundwater for irrigating crops is only one indication of Panhandle farmers' concern about prudently using aquifer water. Some invested in an irrigation system with nozzles only eighteen inches above the soil surface, thereby ensuring that more moisture goes to the crop than into the air. Indeed, it is estimated that through improved application efficiency, the rate of water use per acre declined. At the end of the twentieth century, there were over 2,000 irrigation wells in the Oklahoma Panhandle with more than half (1,213) in Texas County alone. While no precise conclusions can be reached about the endurance of the aquifer, it is already evident to Panhandle farmers that as water levels decline, the cost of pumping increases. Moreover if energy prices increase and crop prices decrease or remain stable, the cost of pumping could approach the added value to the crop it if is irrigated. If and when that occurs, the irrigating farmer will have to determine whether the potential future income justifies the cost. Needless to say, all the Panhandle irrigators are aware of the necessity to avoid reckless pumping.[6]

While most of the current problems and concerns about land
and water use relate in one way or another to the advent of the
huge hog farms accompanying the arrival of Seaboard Farms in
1993, it is clear that, despite its fines and violations, Seaboard is
making strenuous efforts to be a good corporate citizen. Early in
2003 it concluded a lawsuit settlement with the Sierra Club that
will safeguard against environmental impact from its Dorman
Sow Farms. Seaboard completed a major overhaul of its waste
management systems to improve water pollution controls and
agreed to contribute $100,000 to wetlands conservation and
other similar projects in the Panhandle. Seaboard vowed to mon-
itor nitrogen levels in nearby soil, to conduct regular inspections
after hog waste was applied to land, and to allow Sierra Club
representatives to inspect the Dorman Sow Farms annually.
Seaboard also pledged to address water pollution issues at its
other facilities in Oklahoma. The agreement partially resolved a
lawsuit filed by the Sierra Club in July 2000 that accused the
Dorman operation of violating the Clean Water Act and the federal Superfund law. Although Sierra Club officials said the
settlement represented "one of the largest solutions-oriented
agreements ever reached between an environmental group and
an animal production company," the Sierra Club's claim that
Seaboard must report ammonia gas emissions at the Dorman
plant remained unresolved.[7]

The 1991 corporate farming law and the arrival of Seaboard
Farms are at the root of the fundamental transformation of the
Oklahoma Panhandle from a monocultural outback to one of
much greater diversity. To reiterate, when Oklahoma became a

state in 1907, the Panhandle had a total population of 35,739. The 2000 census showed a population of 29,112. Only Texas County gained in population—from 16,448 in 1907 to 20,107 in 2000. Currently more than half of its inhabitants reside in Guymon, the focal point for many of the activities and developments occurring in the Panhandle. The 2000 census further indicated that the nonwhite population, formerly miniscule, numbered 7,118, with 6,003 residing in Texas County. Other ethnic groups, while slowly increasing in numbers, can in no way match the growth of the Hispanic population. The number of African Americans, Asians, and American Indians cited in the census adds up to less than 700 individuals. However, two further census categories, *Other* and *Two or More Races,* account for 5,304 of the population, with 4,175 of these people residing in Texas County. Clearly a fundamental change population-wise is occurring in the Oklahoma Panhandle.[8]

This nonwhite population, including many immigrants from Mexico, finds job opportunities in the growing pork industry, which services growing markets in the Far East and South America. In 2003 Texas County commissioners, recognizing the fact that 33 to 34 percent of the population is Hispanic, tabled a resolution to make English the official language of county government. By 2000 Hispanics made up about half of the total enrollment in Guymon Public Schools and provided about two-thirds of the workforce employed at Seaboard Farms. With hog farm workers making around $23,000 per year with over-time, unemployment is minimal. *Spanish Spoken Here* signs in Guymon storefronts, Spanish advertisements in the press, Mexican restaurants, and Spanish radio programs indicate that homogeneity in Texas County, and elsewhere in the Panhandle though less so, is giving way to diversity. In 2004 Panhandle State University hosted a Mexican folklore dance workshop, an event that would have been unheard of in previous years.

As the new arrivals were being "mainstreamed" and embraced in the community, a world market was beginning to supercede the domestic market for the Panhandle's bountiful production. However, a darker side became evident in the growing demand for social services, public assistance, and housing and in the increasing crime rates. Diversity in all of its manifestations, both positive and negative, is transforming the Panhandle. While the seeds of change can be traced back to the 1991 corporate farming law and the arrival of Seaboard Farms in Guymon shortly thereafter, how long these developments will endure is an open-ended question depending on how long the two basic non-renewable natural resources—natural gas and underground water—continue to respond to the efforts of modern technology to bring them to the surface. The future of this American outback is almost impossible to predict, but it seems evident that the Oklahoma Panhandle has markedly changed over the past ten decades.[9]

Notes

PLAINSWORD

1. See Walter Prescott Webb, *The Great Plains* (Boston: Ginn, 1931).

2. John W. Morris, Charles R. Goins, and Edwin C. McReynolds, *Historical Atlas of Oklahoma*, 3rd ed. (Norman: University of Oklahoma Press, 1986), "Oklahoma Panhandle, 1980," Number 81, n.p.

3. *Webster's New Twentieth-Century Dictionary Unabridged*, 2nd ed. (New York: Simon and Schuster, 1983), 1293. See also Fred W. Rathjen, *The Texas Panhandle Frontier* (Austin: University of Texas Press, 1973).

4. Morris, Goins, and McReynolds, Number 81; Katherine G. Morrissey, *Mental Territories: Mapping the Inland Empire* (Ithaca, New York: Cornell University Press, 1997), particularly 8–20 and 163–66.

5. Morris, Goins, and McReynolds, Number 81.

6. See Webb, especially 10–26; James E. Wright and Sarah Z. Rosenberg, eds., *The Great Plains Experience: Readings in the History of a Region* (Lincoln, Nebraska: University of Mid-America, 1978), 9–13; and Carl F. Kraenzel, *The Great Plains in Transition* (Norman: University of Oklahoma Press, 1955), especially 12–23.

7. *The Heirs to No Man's Land*, film by Scott Neilsen and Richard Blofson, produced by University of Mid-America, Great Plains Experience series, Film 5, Nebraska Educational Television, Lincoln, Nebraska, 1977, 28.30 min.

8. Richard Lowitt, *George W. Norris: The Making of a Progressive, 1861–1912* (Syracuse, New York: Syracuse University Press, 1963); *George W. Norris: The Persistence of a Progressive, 1913–1933* (Urbana: University of Illinois Press, 1971); and *George W. Norris: The Triumph of a Progressive, 1933–1944* (Urbana: University of Illinois Press, 1978).

9. Richard Lowitt, *Bronson M. Cutting: Progressive Politician* (Albuquerque: University of New Mexico Press, 1992).

10. Richard Lowitt, *Fred Harris: His Journey from Liberalism to Populism* (Lanham, Maryland: Rowman & Littlefield Publishers, 2002).

11. Richard Lowitt, *The New Deal and the West* (Bloomington: Indiana University Press, 1984).

12. Richard Lowitt and Valerie Sherer Mathes, *The Standing Bear Controversy: Prelude to Indian Reform* (Urbana: University of Illinois Press, 2003).

INTRODUCTION

1. Alvin O. Turner, ed. *Letters from the Dust Bowl by Caroline A. Henderson* (Norman: University of Oklahoma Press, 2003).

AN AMERICAN OUTBACK

1. My observations of the Australian Outback were derived from A. R. Dyer, *Longmans Australian Geographies: The Northern Territory No. 15* (Victoria: Longmans Green & Co. Ltd., 1962); Nancy and Andrew Learmouth, *Regional Landscapes of Australia* (London: Heineman Educational Books, 1971), 305–15; and Griffith Taylor, *Australia* (London: Metheum & Co. Ltd., 1951), 101–24.

2. For an excellent discussion of the creation of the area, see Kenneth R. Turner, "The Creation of No Man's Land," Brochure Series no. 1 (June 1994), No Man's Land Historical Society, Goodwell, Oklahoma. See also Fred Floyd, "Boundaries of the Oklahoma Panhandle," in *Boundaries of Oklahoma*, ed. John W. Morris, (Oklahoma City: Oklahoma Historical Society, 1980), 73–88.

3. Turner, "The Creation of No Man's Land." For a monographic discussion see Carl Coke Rister, *No Man's Land* (Norman: University of Oklahoma Press, 1948).

4. In my discussion of Panhandle topography, I have relied heavily on Charles Newton Gould, *Travels Through Oklahoma* (Oklahoma City: Harlow Publishing Company, 1928), 18–23, 62–64.

5. My discussion of topography, climate, and early land use was derived from E. P. Rothrock, "Geology of Cimarron County, Oklahoma," Oklahoma Geological Society, *Bulletin No. 34*, October 1925; Charles N. Gould and John T. Lonsdale, "Geology of Texas County, Oklahoma," Oklahoma Geological Society, *Bulletin No. 37*, April 1926; and Gould and Lonsdale, "Geology of Beaver County, Oklahoma," Oklahoma Geological Society, *Bulletin No. 38*, August 1926.

6. Fred Floyd, "The Struggle for Railroads in the Oklahoma Panhandle," *Chronicles of Oklahoma* 54 (1976–77): 489–518. Floyd's article could be considered the definitive account. See also Paul Bonnifield, "The Oklahoma Panhandle's Agriculture to 1930," *Red River Valley Historical Review* 3 (1978): 64–65. A letter in the *Guymon Herald*, February 8, 1912, 7, cites products shipped via the Rock Island Railroad from January 1, 1910 to December 1, 1911. A total of 1,129 railroad cars departed from Guymon, an average of 49 cars per month, while farmers in neighboring counties engaged in long hauls through sand hills to reach a railroad.

7. Hurshal Risinger, "Social and Economic Study of Texas County" (master's thesis, University of Oklahoma, 1937), 59–60, 74–76.

8. *Guymon Herald*, January 2, 1908; Bonnifield, "The Oklahoma Panhandle's Agriculture to 1930," 65–66; *Daily Oklahoman*, February 3, 1907, for profitability of growing cantaloupes.

9. *Guymon Herald*, February 9, 1905; Donald E. Green, *Panhandle Pioneer* (Norman: University of Oklahoma Press, 1979), 60.

10. *History of Beaver County*, vol. 2 (Beaver City: Beaver Historical Society, 1971), 133; Helen Huddleston, interview by the Oklahoma Historical Society, Oklahoma City, August 23, 1986.

11. See *Woodward News*, December 12, 1902, regarding the availability of vacant land prior to statehood.

12. *Guymon Herald*, March 3, 1910; See *Beaver County Democrat*, May 27, 1909, for discussion of a possible dam where the Cimarron River comes out of New Mexico at the extreme western part of the state. In 1910 at this location

the land was more than 1,000 feet higher than most of the Panhandle. See also Dick T. Morgan to S. K. Rogers, May 13, 1920, folder 17, box 20, Dick T. Morgan Papers, Carl Albert Center, University of Oklahoma, Norman, Oklahoma (hereafter cited as CAC). Morgan, though favoring a Cimarron County project, did not believe the irrigation fund under the Reclamation Act was large enough to meet the demand throughout the western states. For further interest in a dam along the Cimarron River and water development, see J. B. Thoburn to W. D. Youtsler, February 16, 1923, and Ira E. Myers to J. A. Whitehurst, May 7, 1923, J. B. Thoburn Papers, Oklahoma Historical Society, Oklahoma City.

13. *Oklahoma State Board of Agriculture: First Biennial Report for the Years 1907 and 1908* (Guthrie, 1908), Part IV, 13; Part IX, 34, 109, 118, 173; *Second Biennial Report for Years 1909–1910* (Guthrie, 1910), 139. See also *Second Biennial Report for Years 1909–1910* (Guthrie, 1910), 18–21, for an extended discussion of the tensions between Texas cattlemen, railroad interests, most Indian tribes, and the Board of Agriculture over its efforts to eradicate Texas fever. For an example of the dissemination of knowledge about making crops drought resistant, see *Oklahoma Farmer-Stockman* April 7, 1913, 3, for a story on Kafir corn, and December 4, 1913, 15, for a story on windmills for pumping water. See also *Biennial Report for the Period June 3, 1914 to June 30, 1915* (Oklahoma City, 1916), 16, for discussion of altitude in Cimarron County.

14. *Guymon Herald,* April 9, 1914; June 25, 1914; October 15 and 29, 1914; and February 1, 1917.

15. F. Hiner Dale, *An Oklahoma Lawyer* (Guymon, 1961), 134.

16. Donald Green, "Beginnings of Wheat Culture in Oklahoma," in *Rural Oklahoma,* ed. Donald Green (Oklahoma City: Oklahoma Historical Society, 1977), 67; *Oklahoma Farmer-Stockman,* May 10, 1917, 15; June 25, 1917, 12; August 10, 1918, 23; November 10, 1920, 8.

17. For the discussion of climate and weather, I have relied on Gould and Lonsdale, "Geology of Texas County, Oklahoma," 10–11; Ralph Bennett, "Winds of the Panhandle," in *Panhandle Pioneers,* vol. 2, ed. Texhoma Genealogical and Historical Society (Texhoma, Oklahoma: The Times, 1970), 66–68; *Cimarron News,* May 7, 1914; John C. Dawson, *High Plains Yesterdays* (Austin: Eakin Press, 1955), 196–97; Norma Young, *The Tracks We Followed*

(Amarillo, Texas: Southwestern Publications, 1991), 63; Lindsey L. Long, "Big Snow 1911–1912," in *History of Beaver County*, vol. 2 (Beaver, Oklahoma: Beaver County Historical Society, 1971), 88–89; *Daily Oklahoman*, November 28, 1930; *Guymon Herald*, August 13, 1925.

18. *Pictorial Edition of the Hooker Advance*, 1928.

19. *Oklahoma Farmer-Stockman*, April 3, 1913, 13; *Guymon Herald*, March 21, 1923; *Pictorial Edition of the Hooker Advance*, 1928. This special edition of the Hooker newspaper put a positive spin on the dust storm in "The Thrill That Comes Once in a Lifetime."

20. My discussion of agriculture was derived from *Lee Nichols Oral History*, Oklahoma Historical Society, Oklahoma City, Oklahoma, 14 May 1985; *Daily Oklahoman*, December 5, 1926, sect. D, 1; J.W. Morris Papers, box 22, Western History Collection, University of Oklahoma, Norman, Oklahoma (hereafter cited as WHC); *Pictorial Edition of the Hooker Advance*, 1928; Gould and Lonsdale, "Geology of Texas County," 62.

21. Bureau of Chemistry and Soils, "Soil Survey of Texas County, Oklahoma," Series 1930, Number 28, (Washington, DC: USDA, 1930), 25–26.

22. Bureau of Chemistry and Soils, "Soil Survey of Texas County, Oklahoma," 8–9. I am generalizing for the Panhandle on the basis of Texas County. The Panhandle had the lowest percentage of tenancy in Oklahoma.

23. *Beaver Democrat*, March 29, 1917, and 4 January 1923; *Guymon Herald*, January 15, 1923; *Daily Oklahoman*, January 18, 1923, sect. B, 5.

24. *Panhandle Herald*, November 26, 1925; February 10, 1927; January 3, 1929; and February 7, 1929; Oklahoma Geologial Survey, "Oil and Gas in Oklahoma," *Bulletin No. 40*, vol. 1, November 1928, 228, 253–54, 274; J. Ralph Jett, "Introducing Cimarron County, Oklahoma," in *The Western Empire*, July 1929, 12; *Daily Oklahoman*, April 11, 1926, sect. D, 5, and April 18, 1926, sect. D, 14.

25. "The Dust Bowl," USDA, *Editorial Reference Series No. 7*, July 15, 1940, 36–37; The Oklahoma State Planning Board, *Preliminary Report: 1936*, Oklahoma City, 1936, is full of agricultural statistics compiled by the Department of Agricultural Economics at Oklahoma A&M (now Oklahoma State University).

THE OKLAHOMA PANHANDLE IN THE 1930S AND 1940S

1. Oklahoma State Board of Agriculture, "Foreword," *Biennial Report 1929–1930* (Oklahoma City: Oklahoma State Board of Agriculture, 1930), 19–20.

2. Vance Johnson, *Heaven's Tableland: The Dust Bowl Story* (1947; reprint, New York: DaCapo Press, 1974) is a good introduction by a contemporary who lived during the Dust Bowl. Three scholarly books, all with *Dust Bowl* as the main title, present different views. Donald Worster in *Dust Bowl: The Southern Plains in the 1930s* (New York: Oxford University Press, 1979) blames a capitalist ethic that stressed enhanced production and reliance on technology that overwhelmed submarginal lands and prevented improved land use. Farmers themselves caused land abuse and soil erosion. Paul Bonnifield in *The Dust Bowl: Men, Dirt, and Depression* (Albuquerque: University of New Mexico Press, 1979) argues that government planners misunderstood the problems of Dust Bowl farmers and generally failed in their efforts. The situation would have righted itself without New Deal intervention. Bonnifield focuses on the Texas Panhandle, where oil wells helped tide over farmers and ranchers with small royalty payments, a situation not applicable to the Oklahoma Panhandle. R. Douglas Hurt in *The Dust Bowl: An Agricultural and Social History* (Chicago: Nelson-Hall, 1981) presents a more balanced view between the positions of Bonnifield and Worster. He claims land utilization programs were generally successful in bringing about a shift away from destructive land uses. An impressive contemporary account by a botanist who traced the origins of the Dust Bowl is Paul Sears, *Deserts on the March* (Norman: University of Oklahoma Press, 1935).

3. I greatly benefited for material in this paragraph from my reading of E. G. Fitzpatrick and W. C. Boatwright, *Soil Survey of Texas County, Oklahoma*, United States Department of Agriculture, Series 1930, No. 28 (Washington, DC: U.S. Government Printing Office [GPO], 1930).

4. While the literature on dust storms is enormous and almost every book and article cited thus far devotes attention to the storms, I am concentrating on land use and efforts to combat conditions prevailing in the Panhandle. A fine unpublished study is Fred Floyd, "A History of the Dust Bowl" (Ph.D. diss,

University of Oklahoma, 1950). For the dust storm enveloping Beaver see *Tulsa* (Oklahoma) *Daily World*, May 5, 1935, and Floyd, "History of the Dust Bowl," Appendix VIII.

5. Information in this paragraph was gleaned from county reports in the *Oklahoma Farmer-Stockman* between September 1, 1931, and August 1934. See also Evelyn Harris and Caroline Henderson, "Letters of Two Women Farmers," *Atlantic Monthly* 152 (August 1933): 238–45. Henderson and her husband, Will, owned the Wayside Farm near Eva in Texas County.

6. C. R. Board to Elmer Thomas, June 22, 1933, Elmer Thomas Papers, Subject A, box 25, folder 7, CAC, (hereafter cited as Thomas Papers).

7. For an account of the Guymon meeting see John C. Dawson, *High Plains Yesterdays from XIT Days through Drouth and Depression* (Austin, Texas: Eakin Press, 1985), 239, and Johnson, *Heaven's Tableland*, 169–70. For evidence of concern by the Hoover administration of drought conditions in Oklahoma see William G. Skelley to Walter Newton, January 23, 1931, and J. G. Puterbaugh to Herbert Hoover, January 9, 1931 (telegram), Herbert Hoover Papers, Subject File –Drought, Correspondence, Herbert Hoover Presidential Library and Museum, West Branch, Iowa. A measure was introduced to finance county farm agents and hire demonstration agents in counties seriously affected by drought. Little came of it, and no assistance was given to the Panhandle counties. I am grateful to my colleague Paul Glad who brought these items to my attention.

8. Johnson, *Heaven's Tableland*, 70–71.

9. I. D. Divine to Elmer Thomas, June 12, 1933, R. J. French to Thomas, June 11, 1933, Subject A, Box 25, Folder 9, Thomas papers, CAC. For a story of families leaving en route to Oregon, see *Boise City* (Oklahoma) *News*, April 25, 1935.

10. H. H. Finnell, "How to Reclaim Wind Swept Soils," *Oklahoma Farmer-Stockman*, May 15, 1933, 3–7; E. F. Chilcott, "Preventing Soil Blowing on the Southern Great Plains," March 1937, pamphlet prepared for the Soil Conservation Service, copy in Resources, box 1, folder 18, Thomas Papers, CAC. See also C. W. Mullen, "High Plains Will Bloom Again," *Oklahoma Farmer-Stockman*, April 1935, 3, 18. By 1935 Finnell had left Goodwell to direct a federal project in nearby Dalhart, Texas, to show that with proper practices, Panhandle

soils could produce abundant yields. For a discussion of the drought see "Damage by the Drouth," *Oklahoma Farmer-Stockman*, August 1, 1934, 5.

11. William H. Sewell, "Construction and Standardization of a Scale for the Measurement of the Socio-Economic Status of Oklahoma Farm Families," Technical Bulletin No. 9, April 1940 (Stillwater: Oklahoma Agricultural Experiment Station, 1940); Foreclosure Record, Records of the Commissioners of the Land Office, Record Group 3-4-4, Oklahoma State Archives, Oklahoma City (hereafter cited as RG and OSA); Oklahoma Emergency Relief Administration, Case Loads, RG 28-4-1, OSA; *Current Farm Economics* 6 (June 1933): 78, 81, for data on the number of farms; Works Progress Administration, Division of Social Research, "The People of the Drought States," Series 5, No. 2, (Washington, DC: USGPO, March 1937): 76–77, for population figures.

12. For the number of cattle in the Panhandle, see Arthur H. Joel, "Soil Conservation Reconnaissance Survey of the Southern Great Plains Wind Erosion Area," U.S. Department of Agriculture Technical Bulletin No. 556 (Washington, DC: U.S. Department of Agriculture, 1937), 65. I added the figures for the Panhandle counties and rounded off the sum from 111,347 to 111,000. See also interview with Mr. and Mrs. Ray Oakley, February 5, 1986, audiocassette recording and partial transcript, Oral History Department, Archives Division, Oklahoma Historical Society, Oklahoma City (hereafter cited as OHD AD OHS).

13. Donald Green, *Panhandle Pioneer: Henry C. Hitch, His Ranch, and His Family* (Norman: University of Oklahoma Press, 1979), 156–157. A map in J. Russell Smith and M. Ogden Phillips, *North America* (New York: Harcourt Brace and Company, 1940), 419, indicates that New Deal agencies (Federal Emergency Relief Administration, Civil Works Administration, Agricultural Adjustment Administration, Resettlement Administration, and Works Progress Administration) spent $175 or more in per capita aid in the Oklahoma Panhandle from 1933 to 1936. The Resettlement Administration, like the Civilian Conservation Corps, had no projects in the Panhandle. See also Paul Bonnifield, "The History of Texas and Cimarron Counties During the Thirties: Depression, Dirt, and Men," typewritten draft in J. W. Morris Papers, box 17, folder 14, WHC, University of Oklahoma, Norman.

14. D. P. Trent to Thomas, May 6, 1935, box 16, folder 47, Thomas Papers, CAC; "Wind Erosion in the Oklahoma Panhandle," pamphlet, copy in box 16, folder 47, Thomas Papers, CAC. See also "A Plan for Providing Immediate Relief from Wind Erosion," in Legislative, Box 26, Folder 76, Thomas Papers, CAC.

15. Virginia C. Purdy, ed., "'Dust to Eat': A Document from the Dust Bowl," *The Chronicles of Oklahoma* 58 (Winter 1980–81): 440–545. In her letter to Secretary Henry Wallace, Caroline Henderson said that she did not vote for the Democratic candidate in 1932.

16. Caroline Henderson, "Letters from the Dust Bowl," *Atlantic Monthly* 157 (May 1936): 540–51, and "Spring to the Dust Bowl," *Atlantic Monthly* 159 (June 1937): 715–17. The letters of Caroline Henderson provide the best overall account of the general situation prevailing in 1935–1936 that I have encountered. An index to Works Progress Administration projects applicable to the Panhandle counties can be found on Reels 21–3-1, 21–3-3, and 26–4, OSA.

17. G. W. Mullen, "Western Farmers Are Setting Pattern for East in Erosion Control," *Oklahoma Farmer-Stockman*, January 15, 1936, 3, 15; "Panhandle Tour Shows Improvements," *Oklahoma Farmer-Stockman*, August 1, 1935, 10. See also *Boise City News*, October 10, 1935, for a story about the WPA providing funds for construction of a small dam in Cimarron County, and October 1, 1936, for a story about improved crop prospects. See also Federal Civil Works Administration in Oklahoma, *The Civil Works Administration Program in Oklahoma, November 15, 1933, to March 31, 1934* (Oklahoma City: The Administration, 1934); *Current Farm Economics: Oklahoma* 8 (February 1935); and *Tulsa (Oklahoma) Tribune*, May 11, 1935, for a story about a 760,000-acre contour listing program in the Oklahoma Panhandle.

18. Interview with Robert Kohler, March 14, 1983, audiocassette recording, OHD AD OHS.

19. Stuart L. Schoff, "Geology and Ground Water Resources of Texas County, Oklahoma," Oklahoma Geological Survey Bulletin No. 59 (Norman: Oklahoma Geological Survey, 1939), 10; *Oklahoma Farmer-Stockman*, January 1, 1937, map, 15, provided data on the fall precipitation, which was of minimal benefit to crop production, especially since July was the driest and hottest month on record, and September 1, 1936, 21. But there also were stories of

improved land use and better crops. See, for example, the issues of April 1, 1936, 11, and June 1, 1936, 4.

20. *Oklahoma Farmer-Stockman*, February 1, 1937, 11.

21. Frances A. Flood, "The Dust Bowl Is Being Tamed," *Oklahoma Farmer-Stockman*, July 1, 1937, 3, 27, and brief stories in the issues of January 15, 1937, 28, and September 1, 1937, 4; see Floyd, "History of the Dust Bowl," 172–73, for figures on improved wheat production. See also Kumigunde Duncan, "Reclaiming the Dust Bowl," *The Nation*, September 9, 1939, 270–71 (Duncan pays tribute to the work of H. H. Finnell in his account); *Oklahoma City* (Oklahoma) *Times*, June 2, 1939, for a story on the irrigation lake; and *Daily Oklahoman*, April 23, 1939. See also WPA Collection, box 40, folder 3, WHC, for an indication of the federal assistance Tucker received.

22. *A Statistical Handbook of Oklahoma Agriculture: January 1949*, Oklahoma Agricultural Experiment Station, Miscellaneous Publication No. MP-14 (Stillwater: Oklahoma Agricultural Experiment Station, 1949), 55, 57, 59–60; WPA Collection, box 39, folder 3, WHC, for clipping from *Oklahoma Plan-O-Gram* February 1939.

23. Data was derived from tables presented in James Wesley Ware, "Black Blizzard: The Dust Bowl of the 1930s," (Ph.D. diss., Oklahoma State University, 1977), 228, 230, 232.

24. Minutes of Public Hearing, Beaver, Oklahoma, October 8, 1940, RG 28, box 2, OSA.

25. *Oklahoma Farmer-Stockman*, November 15, 1940, 21.

26. Kohler interview; *Current Farm Economics: Oklahoma* 17 (April 1944): map, 53, and 16 (February 1943): table, 28.

27. Sam Whitlow, "Building Beef," *Oklahoma Farmer-Stockman*, August 1943, 5, and "Notes from 'No Man's Land,'" January 1946, 25. See also February 1947, 12, for a story about the Panhandle and its "ripe brown wheat fields waving in the glowing sunlight."

28. *Oklahoma Farmer-Stockman*, July 1944, 27, and T. C. Richardson, "Winds Will Blow Again—But No More Dust Bowl," *Oklahoma Farmer-Stockman*, July 1945, 8–9.

29. T. C. Richardson, "Savior of the Herd and Protector of the Soil," *Oklahoma Farmer-Stockman*, October 1945, 5, and March 1949, 58.

30. Angie Debo, *Oklahoma Foot-Loose and Fancy-Free* (Norman: University of Oklahoma Press, 1949), 207. In 1937 there were only 592 miles of paved roads in the Panhandle. See *Oklahoma Farmer-Stockman*, July 1947, 53.

31. See *Oklahoma Farmer-Stockman*, July 1949, 3, for a story about developments in Gate and surrounding country.

32. Stuart Schoff, "Geology and Ground Water Resources of Cimarron County, Oklahoma," Oklahoma Geological Survey Bulletin No. 64 (Norman: Oklahoma Geological Survey, 1943), passim, and United States Geological Survey, Water Resources Branch, *Oklahoma Water* (Oklahoma City: U.S. Geological Survey for the Oklahoma Planning and Resources Board, 1945), 118, 120; Warren N. McMillan, "Deep Well Irrigation in the Oklahoma Panhandle," Panhandle Experiment Station Bulletin No. 64, (Goodwell, Oklahoma: Panhandle Experiment Station, 1944), 2–3.

33. *Daily Oklahoman*, October 31, 1948; Schoff, "Geology...of Cimarron County," 40–41, and Schoff, "Geology...of Texas County," 35–38. In 1937–1938 there was extensive drilling of gas test wells in Texas County. No major corporation was involved. See *Daily Oklahoman*, October 30, 1938, and September 10, 1939.

34. *Daily Oklahoman*, October 3, 1948.

35. Demographic data was gleaned from the *Statistical Abstract of Oklahoma*, 1956, and from the *Oklahoma Almanac*, an annual publication that provides population figures, etc., for every county since 1907.

OPTIMA DAM

1. *Congressional Record*, 70th Cong., 1st sess., 1928, 69 pt. 6:6310.

2. House Committee on Public Works, *Arkansas River and Tributaries*, 74th Cong., 1st sess., 1935, H. Doc, 308, 1, 7.

3. William A. Settle, Jr., *The Dawning, A New Day for the Southwest: A History of the Tulsa District, Corps of Engineers 1939–1975* (Tulsa: n.p., 1976).

4. Optima Reservoir, August 20, 1958, conservation box 4, folder 28. p. 1. Robert S. Kerr Papers, CAC.

5. Optima Reservoir, August 20, 1958, conservation box 4, folder 28, p. 2. In 1950 the estimated cost was $18,540,000. See Kerr to Tom Black,

December 4, 1950, conservation box 4, folder 24, Kerr Papers.

6. Optima Reservoir, August 20, 1958, p. 2, Kerr Papers.

7. Anne Hodges Morgan, *Robert S. Kerr: The Senate Years* (Norman: University of Oklahoma Press, 1977), 48–49, 139–74. Morgan writes, "Kerr had pushed through Congress the most ambitious water development/public works program in the twentieth century" (188).

8. Col. C. H. Chaspering, Corps of Engineers, to Congressman Toby Morris, October 14, 1947, topical series box 2 (Optima-Hardesty), Toby Morris Papers, CAC.

9. Ted R. Fisher, attorney for Canton Dam Project, to Morris, April 4, 1949, topical series box 2, Morris Papers; Resolutions adopted by the Tri-State Chamber of Commerce, November 8, 1949, conservation box 4, folder 24, Kerr Papers.

10. H.C. Williams, county engineer for Texas and Cimmaron Counties, to Representative George Howard Wilson, January 17, 1950, box 12, folder 32, George Howard Wilson Papers, CAC.

11. Concern for underground water depletion is noted in a press clipping from *Harper County Journal*, February 2, 1950. Harper was the neighboring county to Beaver on the east. The clipping is in the Wilson Papers, box 12, folder 35. See also the statement of Leon Field concerning conditions in the region. His remarks can be found in box 12, folder 34.

12. "The State Group Gives Details of Their Optima Dam Presentation in Washington," undated clipping, box 12, folder 34, Wilson Papers. Wilson's testimony and that of Leon Field, who represented Texas County in the Oklahoma Legislature, 1950, can also be found in box 12, folder 34.

13. Fred G. Aandahl, assistant secretary of the interior, to Representative Victor Wickersham, March 23, 1954, box 13, folder 58, Wickersham Papers, CAC.

14. Kerr to Mike Grey, July 18, 1955, legislative series box 30, folder 71, Kerr Papers.

15. Grey to Kerr, April 11, 1956, conservation box 4, folder 27, Kerr Papers; Marvin McKee to Wickersham, April 10, 1956, box 2, folder 28, Wickersham Papers. McKee was president of Panhandle Agricultural and Mechani-

cal College. Also see resolutions forwarded to Kerr by the Guymon Chamber of Commerce, February 11, 1957; letter from Martin Henson, president of the Guymon Chamber of Commerce, to Kerr, February 12, 1957; and letter from W. E. Bush, head of the sales department of Light Grain and Milling Company, Liberal, Kansas, to Kerr, February 14, 1957. All are located in conservation box 4, folder 28, Kerr Papers.

16. Grey to Kerr, March 13, 1958, and typewritten copy of press clipping "Oklahoma Panhandle Cities Request Water Supplies From Hardesty Reservoir," July 15, 1959, conservation box 4, folder 29, Kerr Papers.

17. Frank Raab, executive director of the Oklahoma Resources Board, to Howard W. Penney, district engineer, March 1, 1960, copy in topical series box 2, Morris Papers.

18. C. R. Imboden to Fred Harris, February 18, 1965; D. E. Adams to Harris, February 17, 1965. Both letters are in box 25, folder 22, Harris Papers, CAC. *Why Optima?* (brochure), Guymon Chamber of Commerce, n.d., box 26, folder 1, Harris Papers.

19. Lyda Mayer to Harris, February 25, 1965, box 25, folder 25, Harris Papers.

20. Fred W. Mayer to Harris, February 26, 1965, box 25, folder 25, Harris Papers.

21. B. G. Dollins to Harris, February 27, 1965, and Harris to Ralph Grounds, March 18, 1965. Both letters are in box 25, folder 22, Harris Papers. Grounds was the secretary of the Texas County Information League. Dollins, who opposed this project, was an optometrist in Guymon. See also H. C. Williams to Henry Bellmon, March 30, 1965, copy in box 25, folder 23, Harris Papers. Williams, in writing to Governor Bellmon, favorably discussed the engineering aspects of the project.

22. Col. J. W. Morris, district engineer, to Don Dale, January 25, 1965, copy in box 60, folder 1, Mike Monroney Papers, CAC. Dale was a lawyer in Guymon. Statement of Harris before the House and the Senate Appropriations Subcommittee on Public Works, May 17 and May 18, 1965, pp.4–6, box 15, folder 25, Harris Papers. Also see Grey to Monroney, February 17, 1965, box 60, folder 10, Monroney Papers. Monroney had recently toured the Panhandle,

and Grey, serving as a state representative, wanted Monroney to use his "influence to try to get the Bureau of Budgets [*sic*] to allocate $1.5 million for its construction."

23. Mike Monroney to Dear_____ (a form letter), March 9, 1965, box 60, folder 10, Monroney Papers. For a typical example of the pressure on the Oklahoma delegation, as well as the Kansas and Texas delegations, see the resolution of the Oklahoma Wildlife Federation, 14 March 1965, box 60, folder 10, Monroney Papers. It stressed the benefits of the proposed lake for anglers as well as the possibility of it becoming a great waterfowl refuge.

24. Jackson Graham, Office of the Chief of Engineers, to Monroney, April 19, 1965, box 60, tray 10, Monroney Papers. *Update of the Oklahoma Comprehensive Water Plan: 1995*, Publication 139 (Oklahoma City: Oklahoma Water Resources Board (OWRB), 1997), 92.

FROM PETROLEUM TO PIGS

1. "Guymon: Sweet Gas Capital of the World," undated and untitled clipping, J. W. Morris Collection, box 16, folder 20, WHC, University of Oklahoma, Norman (hereafter cited as Morris Collection, WHC). See John R. Erickson, *Panhandle Cowboy* (Lincoln: University of Nebraska Press, 1980), 6, for gas wells on the Crown Ranch.

2. *Guymon* (Oklahoma) *Daily Herald*, April 30–May 1, 1977, special edition, 11–12, copy in Morris Collection, WHC. See also Bureau of Mines, *Minerals Yearbook* (Washington, DC: Department of the Interior, Bureau of Mines, U.S. Government Printing Office, 1953), 2: Fuels, 320. The 1952 *Yearbook* made no mention of oil and gas in any of the three Panhandle counties. See *Guymon Daily Herald*, September 13, 1953, for a story on the Eva area.

3. *Guymon Daily Herald*, September 13, 1953. See also *Phillips Petroleum Company Annual Report, 1954*, 13, *1960*, 9. Phillips in the 1950s was the largest producer of natural gas in the nation. See *The Farmer-Stockman*, July 1954, 18, 21, and September 1954, 24, 26, for this controversy. The controversy over cutting off irrigation gas by Phillips Petroleum Company and others continued into 1955. See stories in *The Farmer-Stockman*, November 1954, 18A-18B, and

February 1955, 19. Lawsuits initially prevented the corporations from totally cutting off the gas supply from irrigation wells. Oklahoma resolved the matter by enacting a gas-for-irrigation law requiring producing companies to make irrigation gas available for purchase by the owner or operator of land on which the gas well was located. By the time the law was enacted, Phillips was the only company to deny use of gas for irrigation. See *The Farmer-Stockman*, November 1955, 38, 40.

4. *Texas County Irrigation and Water Resources Association, Inc.* v. *Cities Service Oil Company*, 570 P.2d 49 (1977); *OWRB and Mobil Oil Corporation* v. *Texas County Irrigation and Water Resources Association*, 711 P.2d 38 (1984).

5. Beaver County Historical Society, *History of Beaver County* (Beaver, Oklahoma: Beaver County Historical Society, 1970), 560–63; G.C. Walpole to Toby Morris, December 18, 1957, series departmental box 10, folder 44, Department of Interior, Press Release, August 30, 1958, series departmental box 120, folder 11, and Press Release, October 20, 1959, series departmental box 11, folder 7, Morris Papers, CAC. At the time, it was estimated that the Keyes field would probably be depleted in 1985. No plant was operative in 1998 when I visited the area. See also *Oklahoma Geology Notes* 24 (August, 1964): 102.

6. *Oklahoma Geology Notes* 38 (December 1978): 227, 41 (December 1981): 198–199, and 43 (December 1983): 165; Kenneth Johnson et al., *Disposal of Industrial Wastes in Oklahoma*, Oklahoma Geological Survey Circular 80 (Norman: Oklahoma Geological Survey, 1980), 68–69; Kenny Franks, *The Oklahoma Petroleum Industry* (Norman: University of Oklahoma Press, 1980), 240.

7. Mary K. Banken et al., *Oklahoma Oil and Gas Production by Field: 1990–1993*, Oklahoma Geological Survey Special Publication 94–4, Part 8 (Norman: Oklahoma Geological Survey, 1994), 8–9, 15; Oklahoma Corporation Commission, *1997 Report on Oil and Natural Gas Activity* (Oklahoma City: Oklahoma Corporate Commission, 1998), passim.

8. Arthur H. Doer and John W. Morris, "The Oklahoma Panhandle: A Cross-Section of the Southern High Plains," *Economic Geography* 36 (January 1960): passim; Doer and Morris, "Oklahoma Panhandle," *Landscape* 10 (Fall 1960): passim.

9. In the 1970s Beaver County, with a land area of 1,790 square miles, had a population density of 3.5 per square mile. Figures for Cimarron County were 1,843 and 2.2; for Texas County they were 2,062 and 7.9.

10. Boo Browning, "God's Land, But No Man's," *Oklahoma Monthly*, December 1977, 83–84, 87. Browning stressed the exceptionalism of the Panhandle as a region physically isolated from the state, suggesting it might be better off on its own. For the opinion of Hitch and others on cloud seeding, see *The Farmer-Stockman*, June 1952, 16–17, and August 1951, 17, 62, for a letter by Hitch.

11. OWRB, *Oklahoma Comprehensive Water Plan*, Publication 60 (Oklahoma City: OWRB, 1975), section 4: Northwest Region, 5–8; OWRB, *Oklahoma Comprehensive Water Plan*, Publication 94 (Oklahoma City: OWRB, 1980), 63, 73, 153. Estimates in 1988 showed that 205,873 acres were irrigated from the Ogallala and that some 3,200 high-capacity wells tapped the Ogallala region. See OWRB, *Update of the Oklahoma Comprehensive Water Plan, 1995*, Publication 139 (Oklahoma City: OWRB, 1997), 29, 95.

12. John W. Morris and Arthur Doer, "Irrigation in Oklahoma," *Journal of Geography*, 58 (December 1959): 426–27; "Natural Gas Fight is Irrigators' Concern," *The Farmer-Stockman*, July 1976, 11. See also *The Farmer-Stockman*, May 1952, 9, and December 1952, 11, 39, for stories about Panhandle farmers and irrigation.

13. Ernest Shiner, "New Methods, New Crops Mean Changes for Panhandle Irrigation," and "Sooner Summary," *The Farmer-Stockman*, July 1973, 6, 7; "Irrigation Keeps Moving," *The Farmer-Stockman*, July 1977, 13. Pumping costs differed with different systems, with the costs of surface distribution about half that for a sprinkler system. The OWRB, which was empowered to grant water-rights contracts to ensure twenty years of aquifer life through well spacing, metering, and other means of curbing water use, rarely did more than grant contracts. See Rebecca Roberts, "Ground Water Management Institutions," in David Kromm and Stephen White, eds., *Groundwater Exploitation in the High Plains* (Lawrence: University Press of Kansas, 1992), 92–93.

14. OWRB, Press Release, "Demand for Fresh Water Soaring," n.d. [1975?]; OWRB, *1975 Reported Water Use* and *1981 Reported Water Use*, OSA,

R9 58–25–3, for the Panhandle counties. In 1975 groundwater use in Beaver County totaled 66,576 acre-feet, in Cimarron County 75,410 acre-feet, and in Texas County 266,077 acre-feet. Figures for 1981 were comparable: 37,739, 67,699, and 211,784 respectively. Oklahoma's groundwater code of 1972 accepted privatization of groundwater, and the OWRB also considered a twenty-year lifespan for the aquifer. Attempts by the board to implement a maximum annual-yield concept among irrigators prompted an injunction by Texas County farmers against the administrative staff of the board for trying to implement the concept. See Chanrasiri Wijeyawickrema, "Allocation of Groundwater Rights on the Basis of Farmers' Consumptive Water Needs," (Ph.D. diss., University of Oklahoma, 1986), 156 and passim.

15. Optima Reservoir: History of Surveys, Reports, and Authorization, February 12, 1965, box 25, folder 22, Fred Harris Papers, CAC; Statement of Leon Field, February 23, 1950, box 12, folder 34, George Howard Wilson Papers, CAC; Guymon Chamber of Commerce to Robert S. Kerr, February 11, 1957, Robert S. Kerr Papers, Conservation box 4, folder 28, CAC; D. E. Adams to Fred Harris, February 17, 1965, box 251, folder 22, Harris Papers, CAC; Guymon Chamber of Commerce, *Why Optima?*, brochure, copy in box 26, folder 1, Harris Papers, CAC; OWRB, "Update of the Oklahoma Comprehensive Water Plan, 1995." When I visited Optima Lake in August 1998, the brochure available in the empty project office had a notice pasted on its face stating, "The Lake Has Not Reached Normal Levels and May Not Be Suitable for All Types of Boating." See the Optima Dam chapter, starting on page 67 for additional information.

16. Doer and Morris, "Oklahoma Panhandle," 82–86.

17. Ferris P. Allgood et al., *Soil Survey of Beaver County, Oklahoma*, ser. 1959, no. 11 (Washington, D.C.: USDA, SCS, 1962), 42–43; Ralph S. Murphy et al., *Soil Survey of Cimarron County, Oklahoma*, ser. 1956, no.11 (Washington, DC: USDA, SCS, 1960), 27; Hadley C. Meriders et al., *Soil Survey of Texas County, Oklahoma*, ser. 1958, no. 6 (Washington, DC: USDA, SCS, 1960), 37. I have relied heavily on these reports for my discussion of farming and ranching. On playas, see OWRB, *Oklahoma Water Atlas*, Publication 135 (Oklahoma City: OWRB, 1990), 52.

18. Jeff Carleton Alexander, "Case Studies of Land Use Change in Texas County, Oklahoma" (master's thesis, University of Oklahoma, 1992), 38–39, 62.

19. *Oklahoma PEP* (Program for Economic Prosperity), July 1966, October 1967, April 1968, July/August 1973. Competition for the Swift plant appeared in 1969 when a National Beef Packing Plant opened in Liberal, Kansas. See *The Farmer-Stockman*, November 1969, 23. See also Ferdie J. Deering, "The Big Move in the Beef Business," *The Farmer-Stockman*, January 1970, 8.

20. Donald E. Green, *Panhandle Pioneer: Henry C Hitch, His Ranch and His Family* (Norman: University of Oklahoma Press, 1979), 217–18, 235–37, and chap. 9, passim. The Booker plant is in Texas on the Texas County line. See Donald A. Brown, "Mastering No Man's Land," *Wichita Farm Credit Letter* (Fall–Winter 1977): 5–7, for a concise account of the Hitch enterprises in the 1970s. See also William Burdette Cavin, "The Development and Distribution of Feed Lots in the Oklahoma Panhandle" (master's thesis, University of Oklahoma, 1967), 16–17, 27.

21. Jerry Davis, "Vertical Integration Is Growing in the Feedlots," *The Farmer-Stockman*, April 1970, 32–33, October 1971, 10–11; Cavin, "Feedlots in the Oklahoma Panhandle," 14, 38–39, 49. The regional telephone directory for 1997–1998 listed fifteen firms under "Livestock Feeding," six under "Livestock Hauling," four under "Livestock Dealers," and two under "Livestock Commission Companies"; Michael Lewis, "The National Grasslands in the Old Dust Bowl" (P.h.D. diss., University of Oklahoma, 1988), 84, claimed that "some 50 major feed lots were listed in local telephone directories." Most were located along what he called a "feedlot axis" stretching from Hereford, Texas, to Omaha, Nebraska.

22. *The Farmer-Stockman*, April 1974, 9, and May 1972, 32.

23. *The Farmer-Stockman*, May 1972, 32.

24. John Fraser Hart and Chris Mayda, "Pork Palaces on the Panhandle," *The Geographical Review* 87 (July 1997): 396–400. I have relied heavily on this article for my discussion of the new pork industry.

25. Mark Droberstott, "This Little Piggy Went to Market: Will the New Pork Industry Call the Heartland Home?" *Federal Reserve Bank of Kansas City*

23 (Third Quarter, 1998): 79–86. I have relied heavily on this article, which examines the new pork industry in a comprehensive manner.

26. See Doer and Morris, "Oklahoma Panhandle," 87, for 1950 figures. The 1995 figures were derived from the county profiles in the *Oklahoma Almanac* for 1997–1998.

EPILOGUE

1. See *Daily Oklahoman,* September 10, 2001, 1-A, for a discussion of federal subsidies received by Panhandle farmers. For a profile of the three Panhandle counties see *Oklahoma Almanac 2003–2004* (Oklahoma Department of Libraries, Oklahoma City, 2003), 356–57 (Beaver), 374–75 (Cimarron), and 488–89 (Texas).

2. See *Daily Oklahoman,* November 14, 2002, B-1, for a story on Smithfield Foods, Inc.

3. *Daily Oklahoman,* October 27, 2002, 8-B.

4. *Daily Oklahoman,* September 14, 2002, 4-A, and June 20, 2001, 1-C.

5. *Daily Oklahoman,* July 25, 2000, 1-A.

6. *Daily Oklahoman,* April 30, 2000, Special Section, 20.

7. *Daily Oklahoman,* January 8, 2003, 5-A.

8. I have secured the census data from the *Oklahoma Almanac 2003–2004* from the same pages cited in footnote 1.

9. See *Daily Oklahoman,* December 3, 2000, 1-A, and March 12, 2003, 2-A, for two stories on the new wave of immigrants. See also Robert D. Kaplan, *An Empire Wilderness* (New York: Random House, 1998), 247, for a gloomy picture of recent developments in the Panhandle.

Index

The author and Texas Tech University Press are deeply grateful to The <u>CH</u> Foundation, without whose generous support the book series Plains Histories would not have been possible.